PRAISE FOR THE BLACK EYED PEAS

….Hip-hop's brightest popsters!
— Rolling Stone

*"Ya know, Mr. Will, **I don't got to work with nobody. But some-thing tells me to work with the Black Eyed Peas.** But I like how y'all do what y'all do. Y'all got the band. In hip-hop, music you don't see enough of that."*
—James Brown

*"I think **Will's doing wonderful, innovative, positive, great music**…I like what he is doing and thought it would be interest-ing to collaborate or just see how the chemistry worked."*
—Michael Jackson

*"**At no point does Will.i.Am stop writing songs.** If you ask him about a plug-in, he'll write a song on the spot just to show you how the plug-in works. In fact, as Will sits in Black Eyed Peas' L.A. studio, wearing a FireWire cable as a belt and staring at his Apple Cinema Display, it's a wonder he thinks about anything aside from music. He's apt to bound out of his seat and record synths and beats and whatever at any moment. He might even make his visi-tors—in this case, a Remix editor with zero rapping skills, whatso-ever—rap on the spot. His songwriting style is all very quick, and as he well knows, **it fosters many opportunities for 'magic' in the studio.**"*
—Remix Magazine

D0743859

*"The choice of **Will.i.Am, Fergie, Taboo and Apl.de.Ap** to be our Instant Def heroes was easy…They **are setting trends** and breaking away from the clutter in the industry to really stand out amongst their peers…*

—Vic Walia, Snickers' senior marketing manager

"Will's not afraid to have fun with a song, to be whimsical."
—John Legend

*"**No PBS producer could assemble a more convincing multicultural cast**—a black man, a white girl, a Mexican, a Filipino. **And no A&R executive could contrive a sound that hits so many of sweet spots.**… Will has become one of the industry's most sought after songwriters and producers. Crossover superstars from Kanye West to Diddy praise the work of the Peas. Radio programmers and Fortune 500 marketing executives take comfort in their upbeat idealism.*

—Blender Magazine

The Black Eyed Peas:

An Unauthorized Biography

By Jake Brown

The Black Eyed Peas:

An Unauthorized Biography

By Jake Brown

Colossus Books
Phoenix
New York   Los Angeles

THE BLACK EYED PEAS:
An Unauthorized Biography

By Jake Brown

Published by:
Colossus Books
A Division of Amber Communications Group, Inc.
1334 East Chandler Boulevard, Suite 5-D67
Phoenix, AZ 85048
Amberbk@aol.com
WWW.AMBERBOOKS.COM

© Copyright 2008 by Jake Brown & Amber Books
ISBN # 978-0-9790976-4-5
Library of Congress Control Number: 2008926259

Dedication

This book is dedicated to my cousin, Madeline. I'm VERY proud of you for all you've achieved in your young life, and admire how hard you're working toward your future. A bit cheesy of a dedication, I know, but it's an accolade you truly deserve.

Love you,

Your cousin, Jake
June, 2008

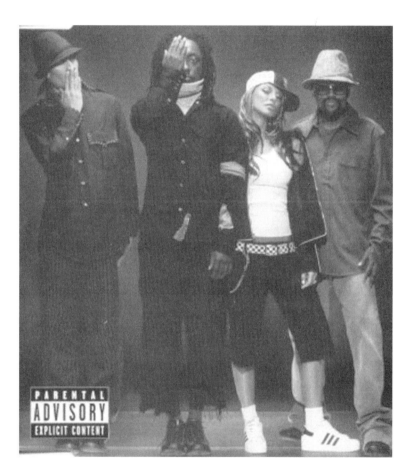

Contents

Black Eyed Peas

Introduction
Global Locals—The Wildly Colorful World of the Black Eyed Peas…

The only question faced by members of the Black Eyed Peas is what to do with all the cash, credibility, and popularity they worked so hard to earn.

—Jake Brown

1

British pop culture has always held a derivative influence over music in America. Most prominent was the British Invasion of the 1960s, which produced the Beatles; the Rolling Stones; Eric Clapton, and the Doors. The influence was so great in the 1960s that Jimi Hendrix, the legendary American rock guitarist and singer, began his career in Britain to gain credibility in America.

The British influence continued to grow through the 1970s, giving birth to the grinding heavy metal sound. As a result, the world saw the development of bands such as Black Sabbath and Led Zeppelin in Britain and Aerosmith and Kiss in the United States.

Later in the 1970s, the British punk rock movement spawned groups such as the Sex Pistols, and the Ramones, and the New York Dolls in America. In the early 1980s, it was British hard rock bands like Judas Priest, Iron Maiden and Def Leppard that paved the way for Motley Crue, Guns N' Roses, among others in America. British musicians continued to have a derivative influence on American music through the early 1990s, including the grunge era.

Hip-hop, on the other hand, had a range of influences other than Britain, including reggae in Jamaica and R&B in America. To be sure, R&B influenced scores of genres. It was made popular by predominantly African- American rock and blues legends such as James Brown, the Godfather of Soul; Chuck Berry; Little Richard; Muddy Waters, and Robert Johnson—who inspired the birth of rock n' roll in America in the 1950s. Much of R&B was popularized by white artists such as Elvis Presley; Johnny Cash; and Jerry Lee Lewis, who covered the work of black artists. Still, many British rockers, including John Lennon, Paul McCartney, Mick Jagger and Keith Richards, credit Berry, Little Richard and Waters as their inspiration.

While Rock & Roll was at the forefront of the music scene in the 1960s, R&B was also popular thanks to the Motown sound, which grew out of Detroit. The sound was driven by talents such as Stevie Wonder, Marvin Gaye, and Diana Ross and the Supremes. The popularity of R&B paved the way for the rise of the undulating sounds of funk in the 1970s, which gave birth to artists such as the plume and feather-wearing George Clinton & Parliament, and Sly and the Family Stone, which later gave way to the development of funk-soul orchestras such as Earth Wind and Fire. Later, the 1980s produced pop-soul icons such as Prince and Michael Jackson, whose music still hold sway over musicians today.

Finally, in the late 1980s and throughout the 1990s, hip-hop came full circle with a new and vibrant, hard-core sound that was made popular by artists such as Run DMC; Dr. Dre and his group N.W.A.; Public Enemy; Notorious B.I.G.; Tupac Shakur; Jay-Z; Kanye West; Eminem. Later in the 1990s, rap moved in a number of directions that celebrated the sounds of artists such as Parliament Funkadelic and even jazz. The influence could be heard through artists such as Guru's Jazzmatazz, Digable Planets, Arrested Development, and the Fugees.

In the new millennium, hip-hop diversified even further thanks to producers such as Kanye West, whose rhythm and rhymes celebrate the sounds of 1970s soul; and Timbaland and Scott Storch, whose futuristic soundscapes cut across all genres. Each of these producers, along with notable others such as Outkast and the Black Eyed Peas (BEP), have advanced the sounds of hip-hop by incorporating a mix of musical genres. As a result, the Peas as a group has reached an entirely new generation of hip-hop listeners. The group's sound is so eclectic that when its music first hit the airwaves, listeners thought they were European. While they may not be European, the derivative influence of Britain on American music over the years has seeped into the core of the very being of the group, from Will.i.Am's clogs to Fergie's smash hit single, 'London Bridge.'

Surprisingly, the group was discovered by Eazy-E, founder of the hardcore East Coast rap group, N.W.A., and C.E.O. of Ruthless Records, who signed Will.i.Am to a recording contract in 1992.

"...Many in the Ruthless camp were puzzled by the group and the enthusiasm of Eazy, who had no problem reconciling his own gangsta style with the peace-minded, break dancing of Atban," according to Billboard Magazine.

But it was about the music back then as much as it is today. The lesson: perfect your art and be ready to perform because you never know when you're going to get your big break.

Now, the only question faced by members of the Black Eyed Peas is what to do with all the cash, credibility, and popularity they worked so hard to earn. The Black Eyed Peas' movement has generated $30 million in album sales over the past 10 years, and as global-locals of the international touring circuit, the group's musical and stylistic revolution can only continue to grow. In the pages of this biography of the Black Eyed Peas, fans will read every colorful and intimate detail of that journey…

Part I:
The Black Eyed Peas-Growing Up…

"…In my own neighborhood, we were one of the only Black families around in our area, the majority were Latinos, a lot of Mexicans, some people from El Salvador and Nicaragua and Tijuañeros. That culture influenced me as a person. It broadened my taste of things that I appreciate, music that I can stand listening to for more than a minute."

—William James Adams Jr.

William James Adams Jr., a.k.a. Will.i.Am, was born on March 15, 1975 in Los Angeles, California, to parents of Jamaican descent. Describing himself as "super-duper hyperactive" as a child, Will was as eccentric as his sense of fashion. His neighborhood in East Los Angeles was diverse, which he says had a heavy influence on his life and music.

"…In my own neighborhood, we were one of the only Black families around in our area, the majority were Latinos, a lot of Mexicans, some people from El Salvador and Nicaragua and Tijuañeros," he told Billboard Magazine. "That culture influenced me as a person. It broadened my taste of things that I appreciate, music that I can stand listening to for more than a minute. Culturally, the way Latinos raise their families, that's influenced my family, from my mom being born and raised there to me being born and raised there. It was just like a little village in these projects where we lived."

Will recalled that as a child, his mother wouldn't allow him to join other playgroups, rather encouraging him to make himself the center of attention. "I'd be like, 'But everyone's playing over there!'…She'd be like, 'So what? I don't want you joining in what they playing. You make something up and make them come over and play with you.'" He later realized that his mother's insistence on individuality helped form his singular style of music and producing.

Though Will was raised around Latin music, his love of hip-hop developed at an early age. By the time he became a teenager, he was a self-described "backpack parking-lot rapper…Those are my roots," he said. Prior to developing an interest in a music career, Will's first love was sports. "My dream was to play football," he said. "If you had asked me from ages 10 to 18, 'What do you want to do with your life?' I'd have said, 'play football.'"

What changed his mind? He took a hit. He describes the turning point: "I was a tailback in high school," he said. "They gave me a pitch and I took the corner and…I didn't pay any attention to the safety coming up to my left. I didn't know what day it was after being hit and I didn't like that feeling."

Will attended high school in the all-white community of Palisades, Los Angeles, where he experienced segregation for the first time. "The black people hung out by the lunch tables," he recalled. "The Mexicans hung out by the bathroom, the white people hung out in their cars, the Asian people stood next to the lockers ... I would always wander between the different sections. If I didn't go to that school, the Black Eyed Peas wouldn't be what it is. I don't think we would be able to relate to every country on the planet."

While attending Palisades High School, Will met best friend and future Black Eyed Peas band mate Allan Pineda Lindo, a,k.a. Alp.de.Ap. Allan was a recent immigrant from the Philippines, where he was born to Christina Pineda, a Filipina, and an African-American U.S. serviceman stationed at Clark Air Force Base. The father abandoned the family, leaving Pineda to raise Allan, his four brothers and two sisters in abject poverty. Music played a large role in Allan's ability to escape those difficult years. He particularly enjoyed songs by the Eagles, the Beatles, Stevie Wonder, and ASIN, a Filipino folk/rock group. When the family picked up and moved to America, it represented a new beginning.

"When I got to the projects Will was living in, I was like, 'Damn, you guys got nice houses. You got toilets... 'Cause in the Philippines, you don't even have toilets," Allan recalled. "It's a different type of a toilet, like an outhouse. We had to pump water out of the ground."

Allan and Will became fast friends. They formed a quick bond over their shared love of hip-hop, which Allen discovered during its invasion of Filipino culture in the latter half of the 1980s. "Will is open-minded," Allen recalled. "He didn't care how I dressed or what I looked like."

Part II:
N.W.A's Eazy-E Discovers Will.i.Am

"I'm a battle MC, don't forget. I got signed by Eazy-E in 1991 just by freestyling."

—*Will.i.Am*

Beginning as a break-dance crew, Will and Allan formed the group, Tribals of the Nations, with a third member, Dante Santiago, a.k.a. Mookie, while still in high school. Steeped in early 80s hip-hop, both musically and stylistically, the trio became a popular fixture at local break-dance clubs such as Balistyx, and at L.A. house parties. Will also routinely won the 'Ballistic' Rap competition hosted by David 'Bud Bundy' Faustino. The group's reputation spread like wildfire. When the smoke cleared, it was clear that Will.i.Am and his eclectic troupe of musicians were star-ward bound.

While honing his talents as a performer, after graduating high school in May 1993, Will.i.Am, decided to attend the Fashion Institute of Design and Merchandising in Los Angeles. After changing the group's name to Atban Klaan, a.k.a. A Tribe Beyond a Nation, the group balanced its wildly entertaining dance performances with dazzling verbal bouts. The performances eventually caught the ear of Eazy-E, the under-rated A&R man and legendary founder of the hardcore Compton-based rap group, Niggaz with Attitude, a.k.a. N.W.A. In 1991, Will.i.Am signed a deal with Eazy-E's Ruthless Records.

"I'm a battle MC, don't forget it" Will said addressing critics who questioned his skills as a rapper. "I got signed by Eazy-E in 1991 just by freestyling."

The group quickly recorded its debut album, 'Grass Roots,' but it never saw the light of day. Label executives could not settle on an appropriate marketing demographic. Still, Will expresses pride in being signed to a record label during a critical era of hip-hop and rap, from 1987 to 1994. "From Shinehead, to Redhead Kingpin, to N.W.A., to Mix Master Spade, to Big Daddy Kane—that's the era that we come from. To me, that's when hip-hop was pure."

Sadly, Eazy E would pass away before seeing his prodigies rise to fame. By March 1995, news of the rapper's infection of HIV, the virus that causes AIDS, was as world-famous as Eazy-E himself. He died on March 26, 1995. With the death of his biggest champion, Will saw his dreams of stardom fade. The group was soon dropped from the Ruthless roster. Undeterred, the trio retooled and formed the group, the Black Eyed Peas (BEP). Dante left for what he hoped to be greener pastures. This regrouping set the stage for the Peas to meet Fergie, who later became an integral member of the flamboyant and technologically savvy crew.

Part III:
Growing Up with Stacy Ann 'Fergie' Ferguson and Wild Orchid and Wild Times …Fergie's Early Years

"I was a complete ham as a child—always performing, taking whatever products were in my kitchen and doing commercials for my dad and the video camera. My parents took me to musicals at a very young age. That was a big deal for me."

—Stacy Ann Ferguson

Of all the Black Eyed Peas, Fergie arguably held the most experience as a performer. As a child, she worked as a singer or stage performer on nationally syndicated cartoons, commercials, and television series. Stacy Ann 'Fergie' Ferguson was born on March 27, 1975 in Hacienda Heights, Calif. to Terri Gore and Patrick Ferguson, who were strict Catholics.

Her show business career began memorably enough when she loaned her voice to the characters of Lucy and Sally on several 'Charlie Brown' specials, including 'It's Flashbeagle, Charlie Brown' (1984); and 'Snoopy's Getting Married, Charlie Brown' (1985), both as Lucy; and 'The Charlie Brown and Snoopy Show' (1985), as Sally..

In recalling the creativity that was inspired by her parents throughout her childhood, Fergie said they encouraged her to act and stretch her imagination. They accompanied her to auditions.

"I was a complete ham as a child—always performing, taking whatever products were in my kitchen and doing commercials for my dad and the video camera," she said. "My parents took me to musicals at a very young age. There was a local community theater and my mom would take me to see 'West Side Story,' 'Oklahoma,' 'Peter Pan,' and 'Annie.' That was a big deal for me."

In a seminal moment, Fergie recalled that her mother saw an ad for 'Karen's Kids,' a group that performed at malls. "She asked if I'd be interested in joining," Fergie recalled. "The group performed show tunes, so it was perfect for me." So, she joined.

From 'Karen's Kids,' Fergie, alongside fellow actress-sister Dana, began appearing as a child-actor in commercials. Her commercial work led to an audition for voiceover work on the Charlie Brown cartoon television specials, where Fergie recalls "Sally's main line was," she said conjuring up the cartoon character's voice, " 'Linus, you're my sweet babu.' "

"And Lucy's was," she said switching to Lucy's voice. " 'Charlie Brown, you blockhead.' "

"Doing 'Charlie Brown' was fun," she said speaking in her own voice again. "It was a creative outlet for me."

Fergie's work on 'Charlie Brown' and other children's programming led to an audition at age 9 for 'Kid's Incorporated,' in which she starred as Stacy, alongside fellow child-actor Jennifer Love Hewitt and pop singer Martika between 1984 and 1989. She appeared in over 100 episodes—all the while maintaining a 4.0 grade point average. Fergie later starred as host of the Fox Family series, 'Great Pretenders.'

The life of a child star was not easy, according to Fergie. "I went to public school, and in the summer instead of going swimming, I would go to the set. We worked six days a week, so I had to be a little adult. I definitely think that's why I rebelled later. Since I was a child actor, I liked to people-please a lot—it's called being professional when you're younger. And I didn't know how to say no."

In addition to acting, Fergie's parents recognized her musical talents and exposed her to a variety of genres from an early age, escorting her to the glitzy and high-octane concert performances of Tina Turner, the Pointer Sisters and Madonna. "But then, I didn't want to just sit there, I wanted to do it," she recalled about watching the concerts. By her late-teens, Fergie did just that. She teamed with former 'Kids Incorporated' cast mates, Renee Sandstrom and Stefanie Reidel and formed Wild Orchid after graduating from Glen A. Wilson High School in May 1993.

At 20, she left home to pursue a full-time music career with the group. She raised her profile and picked up extra cash by working as a model for Bongo and Guess jeans. She also took up acting again, snagging appearances in the popular television series, 'Married with

Children' in 1994; the NBC mini-series, 'California Dreams' in 1995; and the movie, 'Outside Ozona' in 1998.

But Fergie's primary employment came from Wild Orchid, which was first assembled by songwriter Bobby Sandstrom in the early-1990s. Sandstrom later assisted the group in writing and producing a demo that would win members a deal with Sony Publishing in 1993. A year later, the group would sign a major deal with RCA Records, where members met A&R representative Ron Fair. Fair, who entered the studio with the group in 1995 to  produce their debut album, enlisted some of the biggest names in the industry to work on the album. It paid off.

The group's first single, 'At Night I Pray,' bowed on *Billboard Magazine's* singles chart in the winter of 1996, while the video played in heavy rotation on MTV and VH-1. The following spring, the group released its self-titled debut album to rave reviews. *Rolling Stone Magazine* noted that the girls had "much better voices than the Spice Girls." The album's second single, 'Talk to Me,' a respectable hit, was featured in 'Fools Rush In,' a film starring Matthew Perry and Salma Hayek. The album went platinum, with the release of a third hit single, "Supernatural.' The accolades did not end there. The group received two Billboard Magazine Award nominations for 'Talk to Me'; two Lady Of Soul/Soul Train Award nominations for Album of The Year by A Group, Band or Duo; and Best Music

Video for 'Talk To Me'; and an American Music Award nomination for Favorite R&B/Soul New Artist.

The group toured heavily throughout 1996 and 1997, and made numerous television appearances, including on the Rikki Lake and Rupaul shows. The Orchid opened for a variety of groups, including popular boy bands, 98 Degrees and NSYNC. They also opened for veteran pop singers Cindi Lauper and Cher. The group wasted no time capitalizing on its newfound popularity. They re-entered the recording studio in the summer of 1997 to begin work on a second album, 'Oxygen.' By late-fall, the group hit the charts with a new single, 'Declaration.' By 1999, members of the Orchid were so popular that they had their own Saturday morning television show on the Fox Family Channel.

But the hard work was beginning to take a toll on Fergie's emotional health. She developed a brutal addiction to Crystal Methamphetamine, a stimulant that produces a euphoric high. She looked to the drug as an escape from her grueling work schedule and lost childhood. Further, the super ambitious artist felt trapped creatively by Wild Orchid and wanted out of the group, but she did not know how to express herself. She had spent a lifetime as a people pleaser and did not want to rock the boat. Instead, she spent hundreds of thousands of dollars getting high. The drug abuse started to show in her physical appearance. Crystal Meth, as it is commonly know, destroys appetites, Fergie recalled, saying that there were times when she ate "maybe once every two days."

"I wasn't finding any more creative outlets in Wild Orchid at the time, so I went into other realms and other ways of doing that," she recalled about her addiction to the drug, which is manufactured from household items. "When I got addicted to crystal methamphetamine...my weight dropped to 90 pounds (41 kg.). I lied to my friends and said I was bulimic."

As she hit rock bottom, she began to hallucinate. "I remember thinking somebody was inside of my laundry hamper...going to come and get me," she recalled, "so I was talking to the person who was crawling in the hamper...when I ended up on the bathroom floor. I hit rock bottom...Once you get into the drug world, you don't realize how far you're getting until you're that far gone...Finally, I started going crazy. In that moment, I talked to God and He said: 'I've given you all these gifts, so what are you doing?' I decided to get clean..."

Recovery was the most difficult part of her addiction, Fergie recalled. But she was lucky enough to have the support of her mother. "I moved back home and started meeting with people and writing and recording," she recalled. "I never lost focus of that goal...I went to therapy. I still go. I need to. I went to Narcotics Anonymous. I went to Crystal Meth Anonymous. Hypnotherapy helped me a lot. I love it. The first time I went was hilarious. I told the doctor I didn't want to do any of that hypnosis shit; I just wanted regular therapy. The next time I went in, I was biting my nails, so I told her I'd been biting my nails and wanted to try hypnotherapy. I went into the chair, and it was amazing. It completely worked."

Free of addiction, Fergie began to speak openly about her experience. She told her fans that people can pick themselves up no matter how low they go. The artist expressed gratitude that she was able to escape the glare of the paparazzi as she underwent her crisis. Some celebrities such as Lindsay Lohan have not been as lucky. "I think there was a plan for me," she said.

Soon, Fergie and Wild Orchid returned to the studio to record their third and final album, 'Stuttering (Don't Say).' The album soared onto Billboard Magazine's Top 40s Album Pop Chart, and the group starred in a Much Music televised concert special in July, 2001. Though the group was at its peak, Fergie left to focus on her sobriety and to pursue new musical opportunities.

Part IV:
Behind the Front:
The Black Eyed Peas: The Early Years
(1997-1999)

"For Will, it started with his first group, Atban Klann, with MC and break-dancer Apl.de.Ap. Eazy-E signed the duo to his label, Ruthless, but after Eazy's death, Atban's album was shelved and the band dropped. Will and Apl then recruited Taboo, and the trio became Black Eyed Peas, signing to Interscope. They went from playing shows around Los Angeles to releasing Behind the Front in 1998 and treading all over the map."

—Remix Magazine

After the death of Eazy-E, Will moved quickly to form the Black Eyed Peas. The group added back-up singer Kim Hill and Jaime Gomez, a.k.a. Taboo. Taboo hailed from the East Los Angeles neighborhood of Rosemead, and like the rest of the members of the group, he grew up poor. He also was of mixed heritage, with parents of Mexican and Native American (Shohone Indian) descent.

Describing his childhood, Taboo said, "growing up in East Los Angeles, I learned about being comfortable without having money. I learned that happiness was our form of financial stability. If we didn't have money for things like material items, we found happiness through our friends and the community environment, and knowing that you could go outside and play and you didn't need a basketball or the hottest Tonka truck. You had your friends, and it was a village of positive energy...no matter what race you were, you were a part of that neighborhood, and you were accepted."

Taboo was perfect for the newly-formed Black Eyed Peas. In 1997, the team began working on its first album for Interscope Records. Signing with the label was a real coup. Today, it is home to some of the biggest names in the industry, including Mary J. Blige, Eminem and Dr. Dre.

The group also worked on perfecting its dramatic stage presence, which has become its calling card. The energy and Bohemian style of dress has helped draw a wide and varied fan base. That variation has helped the Peas to gain the all-important crossover appeal, which is the secret to their success. It also allowed them to promote their debut album, 'Behind the Front,' on a range of tours throughout 1998 and 1999. They went from touring with Outkast to Everclear, the indie rock group, to Linda Ronstandt, the pop vocalist who peaked in the 1970s.

"The group's more rock-tinged numbers...endeared Black Eyed Peas to a crossover audience and got the trio invited onto several high-profile and diverse tours, including 'Smokin' Grooves,' the Sno-Core tour, the Vans Warped tour, the Lyricist Lounge tour, and a stint with Outkast," Mtv.com reported.

Despite its crossover appeal, the group wanted to gain more acceptance among hip-hop accolytes during the 1990s. "Any time you said 'hip-hop' and 'dancing' in the same sentence, people immediately thought of MC Hammer and Vanilla Ice," Will recalled. "It was really frustrating...I think the problem is people don't know who the fuck we are...They don't know what we're about and why we make the music we make because we're the only group like this."

But Will kept his eyes on the prize. He knew that giving up meant giving up on a dream. "I remember when I was with my ex-girl-friend," he said. " I'd be like, 'Look at that homeless person over there. I wonder what decisions he made to get to that point?' I think if we didn't get through that whole period, then we would probably all be homeless, mentally fucked-up alcoholics, with no way out."

The album the group spent those two years supporting was equally as diverse in its derivative musical stylings as the group's touring bills, reflecting what MTV noted as a "mix of rhymes and riffs, which caught the ear of many rock and rap peers." For the group's creative leader, Will.i.Am, the challenge centered on "how to make feel-good albums with substance, but not come off like we were preaching…Nobody wants to be jamming at a party and be preached to. It's a real fine line between 'Oh, wow! Did you hear that?' And 'This guy needs to shut up.'"

'Behind the Front,' released on June 30, 1998, hit Billboard Magazine's Top 200 album chart. at No.129. The album produced the hit R&B single, 'Joints and Jams,' which was also featured in the hip-hop feature film, 'Bulworth.' Critics took note of the group's diversity. Rolling Stone Magazine branded the group as "the latest crusaders of alterna-rap in a hip-pop world. 'Behind the Front' offers an organic mixture of sampled melodies and live instruments aimed at those of us seeking a little enlightenment with our well-oiled boogie. 'Front' really takes off when the Peas challenge the status quo or indulge their braggadocious taste buds; the trio defends its non-materialistic credo…and meet their party quota…'Front' is not without a few generic-sounding songs…but they don't mar this ambitious effort. Enjoy some soul food." Other critical praise came from mainstream giants such as USA Today, which noted that "the songs are as diverse and intriguing as the Peas themselves. And with all that real playing going on, they don't bother using R&B samples for a crutch. The spicy grooves they cook up have a flavor all their own."

Amazon.com, meanwhile, perhaps most accurately identified and acknowledged the group's sub-genre within hip-hop's larger sound by noting that "the Black Eyed Peas' debut, 'Behind the Front,' may sound thoroughly familiar: like A Tribe Called Quest, they sprout positive, deftly delivered lyrics out of their light jazz, R&B, and funk tracks; like the Roots, this multi-ethnic outfit's three MCs drop science in front of a live band that builds its grooves organically; and at their best, such as on the pop and reggae-flavored 'Karma,' the group can out-Fugee the Fugees." In conclusion, the mothership of all e-retail sites concluded that "we can definitely use more of what the Peas have to offer." Indeed, the rest of the world would agree…

Part V:
Bridging the Gap (2000-2002)

"This one is basically our experience from dropping the first album until now...It's been a lot of touring and a lot of performing so a lot of songs on this album are very up-tempo, energetic, good-time songs."

—Will.i.Am on 'Bridging the Gap'

Seeking a shot at international stardom, the Black Eyed Peas spent the fall of 1999 writing and recording a second album. Will's main goal was to deliver a collection of songs that celebrated hip-hop's cross-cultural roots. "We thought along the lines of music and what hip-hop music has done culturally," Will said. "It's crossed cultures, boundaries, musical genres…With the exception of rock and jazz, it's the most diverse music as far as what it accomplishes and has achieved as far as exposure."

Burnt out from being on the road for two solid years, Will explained that at the outset of recording, the group was in a bit of a creative funk. The songs were not great, Will recalled. "We had a little pow wow and we realized that what we were bringing on the stage, we had to bring to the record."

Drawing from their experience on the road for inspiration in the studio, Will explained that "because we've been on tour, because we know the people we know, because we're happy we know them, we can't let that change how we come across on the record…So the album's title means we're bridging the gap between rock-hop and hip-hop…There are a lot of cats that don't like rock, and a lot of rock cats that don't like hip-hop. So we're bridging that gap."

Though feeling the pressure to deliver a hit with their second studio outing, Will felt it was important to stay true to the BEP's roots. "A lot of times, bands whose first albums I like, the reason their second albums don't live up to the first is because they're in the game to be in the game. And they act it. Their personalities change…We're not going to try to be in the game just because we're in the game. People like us for us, for who we are. Not because we're some crazy-ass freaks." Still, the group did line up a crazy list of guest performers for the LP to bolster its cross-genre appeal, including "Wyclef Jean, the Foo Fighters' David Grohl, Lenny Kravitz, De La Soul, Macy Gray, and Gang Starr's DJ Premier," according to MTV.com.

Will explained that the collaboration produced "B.E.P. Empire,' a single with Gang Starr's DJ Premier, to let people know that the Peas were back. The group's collaboration with Macy Gray—their second—initially was to be a cover of a Beatles song, but the group could not get clearance for the release. Still, undeterred, Will, decided Macy's inclusion on the album was a matter of family.

"She was on our last album," he recalled. "She didn't even have a record deal when she did our first joint, and she's a good friend. All the collaborations are with friends. Even if Macy Gray wasn't blowing up, she would still be on the album." The pair ended up recording one of the album's hit singles, 'Request + Line,' which Will described as an ode to all DJ's who support the Peas. Other collaborations included a track with Wyclef Jean, which Will described as a love song.

Released to retail outlets on September 26, 2000, the album's first single, 'Weekends' was an anthem that Will described as "probably the ultimate party song…Our reason for writing it is to pay homage to the nine-to-fiver, the person that works from nine to five, goes out and buys our records, and buys the magazines to read about their favorite artist." Other collaborations included De La Soul and Mos Def, who the group joined on MTV's Campus Invasion Tour, alongside Wyclef Jean.

Critically, the group's sophomore LP was widely praised by mainstream motherships like MTV, which concluded that the album, "like its predecessor, 'Bridging the Gap' demonstrates the Peas' knack for achieving depth—such as on the uncompromising, gritty 'Get Original' and the funky 'Bringing it Back'—without sacrificing accessibility." Rolling Stone Magazine, meanwhile, celebrated the group for showing "the world that not all Left Coast rap devotees are 'bout blingin', bangin' and bitches: Garbed in boho gear, comprised of various races and stressing positivity, the trio is a pointed anecdote to gangsta and ghetto fabulousness…Bridging the Gap is a more organic-feeling representation of their considerable skills and vision. Uncluttered but muscular production, deft samples and smart rhymes all ensure that the album's power increases with repeated listenings."

Part VI:
Elephunk (2003-2004)

"'Where Is the Love?' dominated radio airwaves for months and earned a Record of the Year Grammy nomination. But more importantly, it may have saved the Black Eyed Peas."

—MTV.com

By 2002, the Black Eyed Peas were in the game for four years, and Will.i.Am for almost a decade. The group achieved journeyman status as recording artists and a solid reputation as a touring entity across multiple genres. Further seeking to celebrate its carnival of colors, Will recruited the freshly sober Fergie to become a member of the Peas, and the group began working on 'Elephunk.' Will described the catchy name as an extraction of hip-hop and the strength of an elephant.

"An elephant ain't the fastest, swiftest animal, but it walks smoothly," he said. "It's fat. It's heavy. Thump, thump…Elephants have a big backbone but aren't threatening. They are powerful, but gentle. You don't see elephants biting a nigga's kneecaps…You can just picture an elephant's movement. That's the sound of the album. We have a lot of trombones, fat basslines, fat grooves, and nice, thick horn layers and arrangements. Just fat funk."

Will saw the album as the opportunity to introduce Fergie as a new member of the Peas. Her solo, 'Fly Away,' introduced her to fans in much the same way 'Killing me Softly' introduced Lauren Hill of the Fugees. The group collaborated with Blink 182's Travis Barker on 'Had to Do It,' which Will said was written in response to those critical of the group's crossover tactics and corporate sponsorships.

"I'm not down with people that judge you on business endeavors," Will said, "when business endeavors have nothing to do with your creative integrity. If we do something, obviously we believe in it. We're not puppets."

Rapper Shaddix appeared on 'Anxiety,' which Will wrote about his real-life anxiety disorder. "I've been having anxiety issues since 1993," Will revealed. "I have panic attacks on stage sometimes. I start gagging. You hold a lot of things inside and they just churn in you and churn in you and churn in you until they blow up."

In addressing some of the album's other singles, Will turns to the bright side with 'Labor Day (It's a Holiday)' and 'Get Retarded', which he described respectively as "the ultimate party song…and a college anthem for the next 10 years." The group also branched out into the Latin market with 'Kama Sutra,' which featured Brazilian singer Sergio Mendes.

Inspired in broader terms by the tragedy of 9/11, which affected every American personally in its own permanent way, for the BEP, according to Will, the event re-shaped the creative direction of Elephunk in that "we had the vocal direction of our songs down… But after September 11th, we switched the direction a bit, edged it up a whole lot. Refined it…The whole idea of waiting for the right time to put out the record gave us all this extra time, and we wound up writing more songs…The whole album is about all of the emotional things we've been through."

Arguably the most affecting of those songs—'Where Is the Love?'—while being the sort of typically socially conscious anthem the Black Eyed Peas had become known for, was unusual both in that it featured Justin Timberlake on co-lead vocals, and dealt specifically with the tragedy of September 11th. In describing how the tragedy inspired the song's birth, Will.i.Am explained that, vibe-wise, "it's like if Marvin Gaye was alive today…It's classic soul, some thinking shit… The world needs this song right now. There's no song like that in urban music, pop music. We're saying some pretty deep stuff, some conscious stuff…and it's got a 40-piece orchestra, so it's some big shit…Initially, Justin said, 'Wow, it's amazing you chose me to do it,' because he was going through some stuff in his life and I was going through some stuff in my life and it just so happens we were going through some thick shit…A lot of the songs ain't about breaking up no more; we got over that…Only one song is, that's called 'Shut Up.' We got out of that heartache."

Elaborating further on the 9/11 ode, Alp.de.Ap explained that "when 9-11 occurred, that just changed our perspective a lot and our surroundings…It made us look closer at everything that's going on in the world, and that's how that song came about." Timberlake, for his part, recalled that "when he played me the track on the phone, I had already started hearing a melody…It was just one of those instances of creative people working together and it just worked out."

The Timberlake collaboration was the brainchild of BEP A&R man, Ron Fair, who recalled first presenting the idea to Will by asking, " 'How would you feel about taking a leap and going more into the pop world?' They replied, 'We don't want to lose our credibility or our fanbase.' I said, 'Well, if you don't take a shot at it, it's gonna get worse, because the backpack crowd are the people who will download the records for free.'…I thought, OK, I'll run the risk of them thinking I'm the corporate record-company pig or some kind of sell-out asshole. And literally off the top of my head I said, 'Why don't you do a song with somebody like, uh, Justin Timberlake?' Justin hadn't done his solo album yet. They said, 'Really? We know that guy, he's our friend. Whenever he comes to town, we roll, we dance, we party, we hang out.'"

Ultimately, Fair felt Timberlake's addition was the magic the song needed to become a hit because it "kind of added another layer of salt and pepper to make it less glitzy and return the balance it struck…It's a mixture of a lot of things. It's a hip-hop record, a pop record, a sing-song kind of nursery-rhyme record and a soulful record. And it's certainly a message record."

The gamble worked. It helped launch the Peas and Timberlake into new stratospheres of pop recognition. The shine came just as Timberlake, the former NSYNCH'er was just beginning his solo career and the Peas received its first smash radio hit. As A&R man Ron Fair reasoned, "it's actually one of the biggest records of all time in terms of its radio spins…Will's fears about losing credibility and his audience base worked in reverse. He actually gained credibility, and people realized what a talented heavyweight he is. He's on his way to becoming the next Pharrell or Outkast. The whole thing is just a giant miracle."

With 'Where is the Love?' in heavy rotation, the BEP embarked on yet another tireless tour. This time, Fergie was along for the ride. She added an entirely new dimension to the group's signature set so much so that it was an amazing journey for everyone, according to Fergie.

"I mean, just the ambiance, the spontaneity, you know, not knowing what's gonna come next, she said. "Are we gonna crowd-surf? Are we gonna bust into a freestyle? You never know. So it's an amazing learning experience and just an amazing journey in general."

Part VII:
The Black Eyed Peas' Launch
Toward Superstardom

"This year, we've been aggressively diversifying our client roster, and signing the Black Eyed Peas fits perfectly into our business model."

—Aida Gurwicz, president,
Cherry Lane Music Publishing

When 'Elephunk,' released on June 24, 2003 it catapulted the Peas out of the shadows into international super stardom. The album sold 5 million copies based on the success of singles, 'Where Is the Love?', 'Shut Up', and 'Hey Mama,' which Will explained came accidentally in the studio. "It was one of these days," he recalled. "I was showing somebody something in the studio. They were like, 'Hey, why don't you do a reggae song,' and I was like, 'Eh, if I'm going to do a reggae song, I want to fuse bossa nova with the kind of bone structure of dancehall but using bossa nova rhythms.' And he was like, 'What do you mean? Bossa nova and reggae don't go together!' And I said, 'Actually, they kind of do. It's all Afro rhythms, just a different emphasis on the kick or snare, but they're influenced by the same thing.' So I was showing him, 'Look, you can do it just like this.' And the song came out like that."

'Let's Get Retarded.' was the group's biggest club hit of the album. It was re- -titled 'Let's Get it Started' for commercial release. The commercial success of the single is ironic because the first version was not clubby at all, according to Will. "The very first version has a gated guitar sound, a lo-fi bluesy guitar melody and a heavy kick. That was retarded…After we tried it, we were like, 'Eh, that was kind of gay.' The second version sounds bassy, bouncy and groovy, but it doesn't have the same power as the commercial version, thanks in part to a last-minute walking bass line. 'We were in rehearsal with our bassist Mike Fratantuno, since replaced by Timothy 'Izo' Orindgreff, and guitarist Pajon, and we were trying to figure out these chords. And Fratantuno was trying to find the right note. So he was just going down his frets, and we were like, 'Hey, what's that?' And he's like, 'No, I'm just going …' And we're like, 'Loop that!' So he does, and then we say, 'Can you resolve that?' And then we're like, 'Hey, George, write some chords to that.' We were just listening to the old version in the car, and we were excited. But then I sang the hook and verse to the fuckup that happened in rehearsal, and that's how the 'Retarded' that we have now happened."

The group signed a deal with Cherry Lane Music Publishing in July, 2003, a reflection of its breakout success. It also was a key to the group's lucrative product endorsement deals. The Peas quickly became the darlings of the corporate endorsement circuit.

"This year, we've been aggressively diversifying our client roster, and signing the Black Eyed Peas fits perfectly into our business model," Aida Gurwicz, the company president, said. "We're looking forward to exploiting the many opportunities for the band's increased exposure that this record promises."

Wasting no time, the group went on tour in the summer of 2003. They opened for Justin Timberlake and Christina Aguilera in a heavily promoted concert tour. By the fall, the Peas had gained enough momentum to tour on their own. They were on a roll that would last through 2004.

The tireless 2-year trek and crossover success was rewared in 2005, with a round of Grammy Award nominations, including for Record of the Year, Best Rap Performance by a Duo or Group, and Best Rap Song. They won for Best Rap Performance by a Duo or Group for 'Let's Get it Started. The album won wide-spread praise among critcs. Rolling Stone Magazine credited the album's success, in part, to party anthems and the addition of Fergie. "The Black Eyed Peas recruited sexy crooner Fergie and ditched ponderous rhymes in favor of smooth hooks, transforming themselves from the world's most boring rap group to hip-hop's brightest popsters," the critic said.

'Let's Get it Started' was the gift that kept giving. It was used widely in a variety of commercial forums, including the NBA Finals that featured Carlos Santana, and iTunes as a featured single. The single also was featured in the popular comedy, 'Harold and Kumar Go to White Castle;' a film starring characters from the SIMS video game; and endorsements for the iMAC G5 computer.

Not ones to rest on their laurels, the Peas were already hard at work on their follow-up album, 'Monkey Business,' even as they garnered a Grammy for 'Elephunk.'

"It's dope, and seriously," Will said of 'Monkey Business,' "I'm not just saying it 'cause it's ours...I like it better than 'Elephunk.' We recorded the majority of it in London for two months, and Brazil and here in the States on airplanes, hotel rooms, bus lobbies, museums, bathrooms." Regardless of the genre, the group was definitely doing big busines, just as Will had always planned. The question was how much bigger could the Peas become as the group's stock continued to rise?

Part VIII:
Will.i.Am In the Studio

"What we've accomplished as a group, it's so enormous, I'm not afraid of messing up what we do. We sell thousands of seats in every country on the planet. You can't get nervous. We're all succeeding in all different parts of our careers. Just because I produce Nas and John Legend and Justin Timberlake doesn't mean it will change the dynamic of the Peas."

—Will.i.Am

As often as they collaborate with other artists, many writer/producers compose instrumental tracks, lyrics, and melody structures alone prior to a vocalist ever entering the studio. It's a method used by superstars such as R. Kelly, Babyface, Dr. Dre, and Kanye West. Will is the opposite. "I write better when someone's in the room with me," he said. "Otherwise, I have no point of direction. When somebody's in the room—they don't even have to sing or play an instrument or rap—I can see what they're gravitating toward, what makes them go, 'Oh, that's great! I like that!'"

A true workaholic by the nature of his genius, Will is never without the ability to produce. He is on call creatively 24-hours a day—whether at home in his Stewchia Studio in Los Feliz, Los Angeles, or on the road. To accommodate his compulsive work habits, he said, "I have a Pro Tools rig that I carry in my backpack…Depending on how good the song is, we go to a studio in that city, but in some cities we don't have that luxury."

Will is so committed to his work that he rarely leaves the studio—not even to relax. "Going into the studio, just being there, and just being around stuff, thinking and solving problems, helps me unwind," he said. "If I'm just chilling with nothing to do, then I'm tense. If my mind's not trying to fix something or create something, I don't know what to do. It just throws me off."

The early influences on Will's musical style are wide and varied. Mario Caldato Jr., a veteran record producer, who released an underground single by Jorge Ben Jor of Brazil, is one of them. Will said Caldato was an influence because he combined different styles of music. One day, he'd work with the Brazilian bossa nova sound and the Beastie Boys in the next. "When he produced your stuff, I liked how he stripped it down and just really captured each instrument for how it really sounds."

In terms of artists who influenced his work, Will cites Sly and the Family Stone. "One of the group's singles in particular, 'I cannot Make It,' gets his creative juices flowing", he said. "He gets different musical ideas every time he listens to it."

Further demonstrating the true range of his musical pallet, Will offers another of his historical favorites as 'Rock N' Roll Nigger' by 70s chick-punk rocker Patti Smith, who inspired Will to feel bold in his music. The sentiment he gleaned from Smith's song was, "Damn, these people have balls."

He has an organic sense of music, which has worked well for him. "Your body makes music every day at a more complex level than the music that we listen to," he said. "Music is nothing but harmonics and frequencies that complement each other over time. Every day your atoms and cells complement each other harmonically, vibrating. You're making music every day. You're not what you look like. You're what you sound like. You just don't hear ya, because it's moving so fast you can't hear."

Will works quickly, which should come as no surprise given the fast-pace of the flow of his ideas. "I try to make a song quick to avoid me being lost in it, 'cause if I'm lost in it, it's never going to sound good, everything is always going to sound sloppy, muddy, [and] tinny because I'm in it. I'm not enjoying it. If I'm making a beat and my mind-set is on fixing it, then it's never going to be fixed…When I'm aware that I'm making something, then it's never right…If you've spent three days tweaking the same thing, throw it away. That's a bad relationship…It's like cooking fast. You want to eat when it's hot. As soon as you start, 'Well, no, uh…' then it's gonna get cold, and it's not going to taste good. So you make it real quick, so you can enjoy it."

Will's signature sound, in part, is upbeat tempos and booming bass lines, which is an outgrowth of his genial personality. "I get real emotional in the studio," he said. "I don't like making dark beats 'cause I get depressed."

Will's positive vibes have produced hit-after-hit not only for his group, but for a litany of mega-stars. The demand for the producer requires Will to be at the top of his game at all times, a pressure that he seems to enjoy. "I love the art form of writing songs. A lot of MCs don't practice that art form of songwriting structure, cadences, melody and whatnot, so I honor that art form."

In revealing some specifics about his process for constructing song ideas into full instrumental tracks, Will begins with a rhythm track. "What I do is come into the studio and mic hi-hat sessions, where I just get different hi-hat, percussion, shaker and cymbal patterns, and then in Pro Tools I can manipulate them into all kinds of different time signatures…I've had talks with people, who say, 'I don't like that snare sound. Why don't you use SoundReplacer?…But there's something about the ambience of the room. You replace the sound, and you're replacing all that stuff. So I just do sound reinforcement. Say a snare sounded like paper—it was flat. It didn't have no pop. I'd just reinforce that snare with another snare on top of it. It takes a long time. You see the waveform, the different peaks, and you match it with different snares on a separate track… And then, all my songs are based off of those sessions."

According to Remix Magazine, when Will is on the road, his production rig includes "his 15-inch Apple Mac G4 Titanium laptop, which now looks like it's been driven over by a lawn mower and has since been retired, a Digidesign Mbox and Pro Tools, an M-Audio Oxygen8 keyboard and Propellerhead Reason software all over the world. Will uses Reason for synths and programs beats from a sound library he's recorded in Pro Tools." Printz, the group's keyboardist/trumpeter, describes his equipment as including "a Moog Voyager. I use that for bass on a couple of songs and most of my color tones," Printz said. "The core bass thing I use is a Korg MS2000. I use a Fender Rhodes. I use the Roland V-Synth as a writing tool in the studio. I use M-Audio and my laptop for putting stuff together on the road."

At one point recently while writing on tour with N.E.R.D., the Black Eyed Peas—in another example of Will's endless cross-promotional marketing savvy—arranged to demo the John Lennon Songwriting Contest and Educational Tour Bus, with co-producer Printz detailing a state-of-the-art mobile recording set-up that included "an HD Pro Tools rig in the back, [and] an LE Digi002 in the front. The studio in the back has a Yamaha Motif module for sound and a P250 piano which is a student piano with vibes, harpsichord, guitar, bass—basic sounds in it. It's also a MIDI controller so it can control the Motif. Then we have some outboard gear to plug in guitars and basses or if you want to take something out of Pro Tools, like a kick drum or snare. There's a Yamaha 02R mixing board. There are 2 Yamaha monitors, 2 NS10s, and a subwoofer. There's a Yamaha DTXtreme Midi Drumset…We have turntables. We have Final Scratch. It's cool. We've actually made use of the entire back part [of the bus]. Our drummer's come in, and he's played. We sampled his sounds, put them in the drum kit and had him play the kit. It sounds pretty damn good. Because you get his feel and his actual drum sounds, but a little tighter…Then the front lounge of the bus is just a mini version of the back. There's no drum set, no guitar amps. But we have the Yamaha Motif, some outboard gear, [with] two flat screens so you can split up the Pro Tools windows."

While at home in the states, Will has made regular use of the bus over the past few years, writing both for the Black Eyed Peas, as well as other artists, including Justin Timberlake, the Rolling Stones, The Game, John Legend, Fergie, Snoop Dogg, P. Diddy, NAS, Mary J. Blige, Carlos Santana, Busta Rhymes, Pussy Cat Dolls, Macy Gray and 50 Cent.

Part IX:
Will.i.Am In the Studio (2): Stepping Outside of the B.E.P.

"I finished four songs for Kelis' record, three songs for Justin Timberlake's record, four songs for John Legend's album, [and] 10 songs on Fergie's record. I finished two songs for Nas, three songs for Snoop, two songs for The Game, scored half of a movie, and 10 songs on Macy Gray's record."

—*Will.i.am*

In deciding how to divvy up his creative ideas between the Black Eyed Peas and outside collaborations, Will explains that it's a fluid process due to the frequent intersection of work and travel for the Peas and his collaborators. Offering an example, Will cites the BEP hit 'My Humps,' which he first had the idea for while doing horns for Earth, Wind and Fire. "In the middle of the session," he recalled. "In 10 minutes, I just did that beat—boom, boom, boom—and I breathed on the mike. Played a little synth on it, and that's it…It's a beat with a synthesizer. Here I am arranging horns for Earth, Wind and Fire and here comes [the] one that got people going. "

Will's diverse resume of collaborations—and even his song ideas—are oftentimes influenced by his travels. "Our music lends to all different types of ethnicities and cultures because we incorporate different cultural experiences into our music." During one trek through Europe, Will took advantage of the moment to schedule a collaboration with Sting, and record a re-make of 'Englishman in New York' from the pop legend's 1987 'Nothing Like the Sun' album.

"We recorded the song in Hitler's old studio for recording propaganda records," Will recalled of the song that was recorded in Berlin. "It's all the original equipment from when it was originally put in… It was mad eerie. You don't understand how big this facility is. They got a room as big as a basketball court- that's just filled with organ pipes and one organ. It's bigger than any basketball gym. It's just got organ pipes and microphones in it. This facility is huge…So we recorded a song called 'Union'. It's weird because we're talking about the opposite of what Hitler was talking about- in the same studio."

Offering an example of his usual producing schedule, Will recalled a Prince-like schedule in 2005. "We had a real intensive Asian tour in August, and before that tour, we were touring Europe. Before Europe, we were touring America, and we don't stop touring…I finished four songs for Kelis' record, three songs for Justin Timberlake's record, four songs for John Legend's album, [and] 10 songs on Fergie's record. I finished two songs for Nas, three songs for Snoop, two songs for The Game, scored half of a movie, and 10 songs on Macy Gray's record. All this from January to now, including four tours around the planet. And I filmed and scored the 'Instant Def' digiseries...and three songs on Ciara's album."

Michael Jackson is perhaps one of Will's most prized collaborators. Will thought Jackson's initial request to work with him was a prank. "He called me on the phone and asked me to get down with him...I didn't think it was him at first. I thought it was somebody joking around...I hear 'Hello it's Michael' and I was like 'Yeah right, stop playing!'...He was like, 'Nobody ever believes it's me,'...I was like, 'No, seriously, who is this?' He says, 'It's Michael Jackson. This is me...I want to congratulate you on all your success, you're doing a powerful thing for the world with your music and staying true to what you believe in. I've been following you for a long time... do you mind if I call you in a couple of days at 4pm?' Then he started ringing me everyday at 4 p.m. We were on tour with The Pussycat Dolls at the time, so I started working on music for him on the bus."

Will portrays Jackson as "the smartest dude I ever met. I met James Brown, had the opportunity to work wit' him too. You get a couple of great people to help you live your life. You got your Michael Jacksons, your James Browns, Princes, Nat King Coles, just to shed light on the earth... This is like, a dream come true for me, you know."

Jackson, for his part, explained that he was drawn to Will due first to the fact that "I think he's doing wonderful, innovative, positive, great music...I like what he is doing and thought it would be interesting to collaborate or just see how the chemistry worked." Once the two met, Will recalled, "it was cool. I spent the whole first day asking him questions like 'What was it like when you first did the moonwalk, how did it feel?' It turned into a freakin' interview; everything we're doing today is like branches from his tree. The seed came from Michael Jackson and James Brown. Michael told me for him, his influence was James Brown all the way. I was like 'Damn, I worked with James Brown!' 'He said 'You worked with James Brown, I always wanted to work with James Brown...' I said, 'Ok let's do it...' So those were the kind of things that gave me confidence to move forward."

Once the topic turned to Jackson's comeback and specifically the material the producer would be creating with him, Will explained that he came at the process from the perspective of a fan in context of "how would I like Michael to sound now. What would I want him to do? When I finally sat down with him, I was nervous. I couldn't be the way I would be like when I'm with Justin or Nas. I've idolized Michael my whole life. I had to be honest with him. I told him it was hard and he asked why, so I explained I didn't grow up listening to Justin's music, so it's easy to work with him. We're equals and when you're in the studio with someone you have to be equal, never above or below. When I worked with Nas, I wasn't like 'Ok, here's the greatest lyricist.' You have to put yourself on the same place and make sure you complement or better the stuff you love. I had to really get over it with Michael."

Once the awe wore off and the pair got down to the business of creating music together, Jackson explained that the process began through the singer's routine of taking "sounds and [putting] them on a microscope and just [talking] about how we wanna manipulate the character of it." From that foundation, Will focused next on capitalizing on Jackson's legendary vocal power. "He still sings like a bird," Will said. "He could go anywhere."

Another important aspect of Will's collaboration with Jackson involved thematically discussing the legend's sound in the context of present-day marketing—a norm for the producer in any collaboration. "How are you gonna compete with 'Thriller?' I said, 'Michael, when you wake up in the morning how do you compete with yourself?... He was like 'Oh God bless you,' but I said, 'No seriously, I'm not trying to compliment you Michael, I need to know this for when we get in the studio 'cause the music has to represent that...' Me and him had this deep conversation and started talking about the experience today; ringtones, the computer, iTunes, movies, YouTube, MySpace."

Will's savvy as a producer from the perspective of an artist brings an edge to his collaborations, which draws artists to him. Longtime collaborator Macy Gray said about Will: "He is a very innovative, really creative person, really broadminded…He'll produce a record and the next one he does is totally different, you know? At the same time, though, he's very smart, very visionary. He's not just thinking about your record, he's thinking about the album, how it's going to be perceived, and how it's going to relate to the world. So I learned that from him. He's always looking for the big picture."

Will took another opportunity at reinvention by working with one of his idols, Sergio Mendes, the legendary Brazilian lounge singer. Will pulled out all of the stops while producing Mendes' album, 'Timeless.'

"When I first got with Sergio, he was like, 'Who do you want to put on the record?' I was just 'hoop dreaming,' like, 'Yeah Justin Timberlake, I wanna get Stevie Wonder, I could get Q-tip, I could get John Legend.' All the people I said I can get I ended up getting, but it was all out of luck. It was all out of timing." He also recruited Stevie Wonder, Erykah Badu, Jill Scott, India.Arie, the Roots, Chali 2na from Jurassic 5, and dancehall star Mr. Vegas.

Explaining what attracted him to the challenge of updating Mendes' sound, Will began with how he felt Mendes' had first aided the Black Eyed Peas' early in its early career. "He collaborated with us on 'Elephunk.' He played piano on the song 'Sexy,' which is an inter-pretation of an Antonio Carlos Jobim song. Sergio is great, and we were really on the same plane. He's hip…For those who don't know, he's like the ambassador of Brazilian samba, bossa nova music."

Among Will's favorite tracks on the album, he began by citing one where "I have Sergio Mendes, Pharoahe Monch and Justin Timberlake on a track…Who would have ever thought of that combination? I mean this record is beautiful. It ain't like a club record where it's like, 'Oh, oh this muffin,' and next year it's like whatever, you wait for the next club record. This is like classic beautiful melodies…It's relaxing. It's the make love slow record."

While working with Mendes, Will also logged studio time with Timberlake to develop the singer's sophomore solo LP, 'FutureSex/LoveSounds.' It was a follow-up to their successful collaboration on the pop star's debut LP, 'Justified.' Will and Timberlake first encountered one another when Will was in the studio working on an India.Arie song. "Everyone was listening to it and Justin walks in," Will recalled. "He was like, 'Wow, let me get down.' I asked him if he wanted to do that song and he said, 'Yeah man I love this stuff.' I was like, damn, OK!'"

Years and multiple hits later, Will.i.Am and Timberlake seemed to hold one another in equal revere and regard. "Justin produces great vocals. I never had to say, 'That harmony you got right there is clashing, the fifth harmony you added is making everything sound dissonant.' I never had to say that to him. He just needs someone to press buttons…That dude is dope man…He plays drums, he plays the bass, he plays the keys, he writes and he sings his ass off… and he can produce. So he's more like Prince than anything. I'm not talking about the music, not the obvious Prince, the genius side of things. He's like Prince, dude… He can go in a studio by himself, no producer, a drum kit, a keyboard, a guitar and make songs. It's very rare people can do that these days."

Another long-time collaborator Will holds great affection for is Macy Gray. He describes the artist, who also produces, as family. "I remember hanging out at the studio watching her record, being inspired like, 'Wow…' I try to say goodbye and I choke. I was there while she recorded that and I remember what it felt like."

In helming Gray's comeback album—his specialty—Will said, "I'm psyched about this one because I get to flex my production skills on something totally different...I did the Game thing, then the Nas thing, the Fergie thing, the Sergio Mendes thing, but Macy Gray is a different thing. It's contemporary soul. I studied Natalie Cole's production, Anita Baker's production, Barry White's production, and then applied it to Macy Gray's album."

Will's specific approach to capturing Gray's sound was one in which "she had the same musicians, the mics didn't move on the drum kit, the mics didn't move off the organ, it was the same thing every day...So I told her this is how I want it done, [the] same musicians, mics, same room, and I want it to sound like an album. I don't wanna have to search for hits, 'cause if we just have fun in the studio or make songs, then those hits will come. Nowadays, what's a hit anyways?...It's like, 'Macy, you been gone for a long time, people think you're crazy, that's the kind of record you gotta make...You gotta answer a lot of these people's questions on what they think about you and that's what the record should be about. She was like, 'I get it, I love it.'"

Demonstrating the lengths of his commitment to resurrecting Gray's career commercially, Will even put his own money behind the effort, revealing that "she's on my label, and this is the one that I think will really do it for her."

The aforementioned collaboration with rapper Game was an opportunity for Will to return to his urban Los Angeles roots, recalling the genesis of the pairing as originating with "my boys being...like, 'Game is coming by the studio.'...I had been working with John Legend. All I got is soul stuff. I gotta do something real fast...Let me make a beat that sounds like it could be on Amerikkka's Most Wanted...I study hip-hop."

Game, for his part, recalled that initially he was skeptical, explaining that "with the Black Eyed Peas, I was thinking that Will had changed his sound and he wasn't really delivering to hip-hop cats like me. I respect what he do, but I didn't know if we were going to gel. I didn't know if he could channel that Ruthless energy again…But when I got to the studio, I could kinda hear the bass line coming through the soundproof doors…I opened the door and all I heard was 'Nigga, nigga, nigga—Compton!' Soon as I heard that shit, I was sold. I didn't even shake anybody hand."

Another hip-hop collaborator that Will found exciting to work with was East Coast hip-hop legend P. Diddy. "I loved his open-mindedness and willingness to try something cool," Will said of Diddy. "He just wanted to vibe with me in the studio."

In addition to his collaborations with other hip-hop artists, Will has amazingly found time to produce a pair of solo albums, including the motion picture soundtrack for 'Lost Change' in 2001, '2003 Must B 21,' and 'Songs About Girls' in 2007.

Contrasting his solo endeavors, Will said, "The whole mind-set on 2001's Lost Change and 2003's Must B 21 was if it takes longer than a week, don't put it out…If it's not done that day, throw it away and that was just it. It's not for radio, it's not for video, it's just for us to go out and make music that says, 'Oh wow, rewind that part, you wanna hear that!' That kind of stuff…It wasn't really supposed to sell a lot. The only people I really cared about listening to it and liking it was the Okayplayer community and the Breakestra community. That's not really a lotta people – it's just tastemakers, people that care about music integrity. That's pretty much all I cared about."

In the spirit of the audio-visual blend of his 2001 soundtrack-solo album, and given the freedom and expanded opportunities his new success has afforded him, Will composed his second solo effort as a theatrical score of sorts. "When I tour the album, I'm touring in theaters…So when you see the film, I'm gonna be scoring the music to the film while you see it. So I'm not gonna play shows at regular venues, I'm playing at like the theaters of the world. It'll be in theaters, but not traditionally. I try not to do things traditionally."

Will's propensity for thinking creatively and commercially outside of the box has been a key ingredient to his recipe to success. With the unique combination of an ear-and-eye approach to production, Will caught the ear of Jimmy Iovine, the legendary chairman of Interscope Records. "I knew Will would be a great producer from the first day I met him," Iovine recalled. "It's what you hear in Dr. Dre's records, or Pharrell's, or Kanye West's [music]—you hear great record-making, records that sound different from everyone else's."

Will constantly strives to produce something new as part of all of his musical productions. He also revealed that a great part of his satisfaction comes from the approval of his forefathers.

"The funny thing is that I'll run into DJ Premiere or these dudes that we all look up to—the De La Souls, the Tribe Called Quests—and they all congratulate me and appreciate how far we took hip-hop," he said. "They don't see it as not being hip-hop. They see it as, 'Yo, you guys are keeping it alive.' The fan always has a different perspective than the architects." By this point in his career, Will has become one of the lead architects of hip-hop's new millennium sound, and his future couldn't be brighter.

"From Elephunk came 'Where is the Love?,' a single featuring Justin Timberlake which became the Black Eyed Peas' first major hit, peaking at No. 8 on the U.S. Hot 100. For 6 weeks, it was No. 1 in the UK where it was the biggest-selling single of 2003. The single had similar results in Australia, staying at No. 1 for 6 weeks as well. The album subsequently spawned 'Shut Up,' which peaked at No. 2 in the UK and topped the charts in many other European countries, including France and Germany., as well as Australia, where it held the No. 1 spot for 3 weeks. 'Elephunk' won worldwide success and went Gold and Platinum in the U.S., U.K., Germany, and other European markets," according to an entry in the free online encyclopedia, Wikipedia.

Part X:
Blowing Up

"The hardest thing to adjust to is the disrespect. We are accomplishing a bunch of things. But, because nobody gave birth to us—Like, 'Yo, we came from this camp, or that camp.' Jay-Z, Puffy, Suge Knight did not put us on. We did not come from nobody. So, because a mega-figure did not put us on, it seems like nobody can really relate. That's been the hardest part for me as a Black person. BET and The Source only cover one style of Hip-Hop. The hardest part is Black people not being able to relate to another Black person who has done a lot globally."

—Will.i.Am

Given that Will always had a global plan for the Peas, the group began to work on maximizing its international exposure. To Will, there seemed no such thing as too many tours, interviews or commercials. But some fans and music critics had different opinions.

"A lot of fans are like," Will said, " 'I love the Black Eyed Peas. Y'all so positive.'…Then as soon as you're on 'TRL,' they're like, 'I hate y'all. Y'all sold out.' I don't understand what selling out means. If I changed what I was talking about, now I treat women like bitches or now I hate white people or now I hate black people, that's a sellout. But if you just get recognized for the things you do or the song the record label chooses as a single, which you have no choice over, is not your hard, aggressive one, I don't see how that's selling out…I like Dr. Pepper. I think it tastes good. Just 'cause we did a commercial, it doesn't mean we selling out. I had to do that shit. I have a family to take care of…We don't do anything that doesn't fit with the music…We kinda lend ourselves to benefits so we did the Democratic National Convention to get people out there to vote. And then we'll do a Best Buy commercial 'cause they sell music. Then we did the first iTunes commercial. We did the NBA 'cause it's like, who's not gonna do the NBA?"

Continuing, Will.I.Am explained that "we did the Super Bowl, 'cause who ain't gonna do the Super Bowl? And if they asked you to do two years at the Grammys, you ain't gonna do it? And then we did the Emmys 'cause they said, 'Ain't nobody ever did the Emmys.'…We're just trying to push boundaries, but a lot of times when you are the first, you get flak for it…People say 'sellout.' That's one thing I don't get. That's some dumb shit, because it's like we ain't frontin'. I ain't got crazy gold or being something that I'm not. A sellout is somebody who's one way with their mom, and then when they with their homies, it's some totally different dude…our videos are commercials, and the product that you're selling through that commercial is your album, and the brand that owns that product is a record company. The only difference is that the only place they play that commercial is on MTV, and MTV gets paid all the money from the ads."

Relying on a strategy of independent thinking, which had guided him for over a decade to the upper echelon of the entertainment business, Will further reasoned that "at some point, you've just gotta cover your ears and not listen to the 'he said', 'she said' and the commentaries about the moves you make when you have to make those moves to survive in a business that's sinking. It has nothing to do with getting paid—it's about reaching new listeners through this new form…It's not a messed-up situation, it's just about new media outlets. I have a lot of ideas about that! When you go get your money at the bank and there's a TV screen right there on the ATM, at some point somebody is going to infiltrate that and make a deal to play their music while people are taking their money out. When you're pumping gas and watching the numbers go by, it takes 10 minutes; you might as well listen to a song!…The reality is the only thing they can say about the Black Eyed Peas is 'Those dudes is all over the place,' and that all relates to the fact that we work hard. So if we're criminals for working hard, then lock me up."

Elaborating on their long climb out of abject poverty, Alp.de.Ap put a more basic spin on why his group chased down every opportunity. "For me, personally, I was adopted from the Philippines and my main goal was to help out my family, and I never expected to be this big. But at the same time, we've put in a lot of hard work and we played everywhere when we started and put everything into it."

Will saw the group's efforts as taking hip-hop to a higher level. "Hip-hop was never supposed to stay in the South Bronx," he said. "It's whole purpose was to be the biggest form of music in the world and do the things that we're doing…You think outside the box, and you realize the sky is not the limit…Run DMC would never have made a song called 'My Adidas'—muthafuckas didn't get a dime for it. They were selling Adidas and Adidas didn't even have to do a marketing campaign. They didn't have the little marketing meeting—'let's get these black guys to sell our shoes with laces that aren't suited to fit the shoe and have all these urban kids buy our gear'… These corporations—Nike, Sprite, Coke, Panasonic, Motorola—they're gonna utilize urban music anyway to sell their product because most urban people buy these products. Every rapper talks about Motorola in their video for fuckin' free. So why not get paid for a commercial when people are doing it for free anyway? Why not give it back to Hip-hop?"

Elaborating even further, the front man for the Peas reasoned that if "Coke is gonna get some corny dude from the suburbs that don't really know about hip-hop history, and he's gonna be rapping on TV selling Coke, why not the Roots? Do they not deserve it? I'm pretty sure they got Coke in their muthafuckin' dressing room. Why not [have] the Black Eyed Peas do a Dr. Pepper [commercial]? We're the only muthafuckas that like that soda. I don't see nobody drinkin' no Dr. Pepper in no video. We're an odd ass group. Why not us? I don't understand why people hate. Artists are not making as much money on record sales as they used to because of the Internet…So many people get the stuff off the internet and it's the same damn quality. Artists are gonna have to scrounge up new ways of making money to make music for these fans. What do you expect groups like us, J5, and the Roots to do when we ain't gettin' record sales to give you the music that you like? Y'all muthafuckas better be happy because that way we can take more risks creatively."

Part XI:
B.E.P. Becomes a Global Brand

"The world needs culture.... if you don't understand culture, then you don't understand people. If you don't know what's going on in the world, you're short-sighted...That's what I want the world to do, is celebrate culture."

—Taboo

With hip-hop in its most glorious corporate age by the middle of the millennium, the Black Eyed Peas had no problem becoming the darlings of the advertising/branding industry, especially given the edge members had with their message of positivity. Philosophically at the core of the Black Eyed Peas' musical constitution, the group seemed also to view their newfound success as an opportunity to further push the latter theme into hip-hop's mainstream, combating its typically violent labeling.

By positioning themselves as the chief spokesmen and advocates of all things upbeat, the Peas for the moment seemed to have a corner on the market. "I'm more optimistic on people just getting into hip-hop music," Will said. "This is more of what I want to see for the world: I don't want rappers or athletes or models—I ain't playa hating them, but this is just how I feel—to make more money than professors and doctors. I don't want religion or government to control the people...there should be knowledge, education instead of entertainment first. I don't want people to only come together in times of crisis. If everybody came together just to come together at all times, there would be no need to just come together in the time of crisis."

Elaborating, Alp.de.Ap reasoned that "there should be equal treatment for everybody. That would stop certain jealousies from other countries. People that hate America ... I think if America really helped other countries out and didn't try to take everything, it would be cool. Equal treatment is what I hope for." Taboo, for his part, felt that "the world needs culture. The whole thing about people hating on Muslims, people hating on Middle Eastern people ... if you don't understand culture, then you don't understand people. If you don't know what's going on in the world, you're short-sighted...That's what I want the world to do, is celebrate culture."

Will's discipline on positivity was so honed in context of the Peas' message that the group even avoided profanity in large part on their records. "We don't really cuss that much...I mean we cuss amongst each other but mine, like, turns off when I'm around my mom. Automatically, it turns off. My mom told me that your words make you what you are, they're the result of how you respond to things, emotionally and constructively, so you might as well have a whole bunch of good words in your head to describe how you feel in given situations."

Key to getting that message out, beyond the media element of their press coverage and constant endorsement presence across every conceivable product frontier was an equally as global presence on the touring circuit. Long the BEP's bread and butter, their show was now in greater demand than ever before, and the group took international advantage by supplying a mix of paid and charity live concert dates that kept them on the road for much of 2004 and 2005. The balanced blend of paid and free shows were key to maintaining the BEP's credibility as arguably hip-hop's most enlightened ambassadors to the broader world. On the not-for-profit front, for instance, the BEP in May, 2005 performed for 60,000 fans at Johannesburg Stadium in South Africa on behalf of the Shanduka Foundation and the Adopt-a-School program.

Utilizing the event to simultaneously launch their philanthropic foundation, the Peapod Foundation, the Black Eyed Peas attracted luminaries such as Nelson Mandela and Oprah Winfrey. According to Fergie, the group's international travel inspired them to found the charity, explaining that "we fly all over the world doing concerts everywhere, and you see a big golf course and it's all beautiful and in the next block you see cardboard houses, and it's just inhumane if you don't do something about that or feel obligated to help in some way...Some of these kids have never even seen a show in their life, and they're gonna get to go see a concert- so it's a beautiful thing."

Elaborating, Will.i.Am explained about the group's charitable efforts in South Africa, "What we're doing there is to bring good music and to have a good time with these people. That's our gift to South Africa. The school that Nelson Mandela is a part of, it's the grand opening of that university, so we're there to celebrate that as well…We're gonna ask kids what their dreams are and hopefully put together a nice little presentation and air it on television so people in America can see it…And other artists can go out there and pick other Third World countries to do the same efforts for."

In addition to the reward the group seemed to experience from their charity touring events, the pure act of touring itself- aside from the millions of dollars they earned- seemed to be the greatest reward for the BEP, allowing them to stay connected to a fan base they had allowed to guide their career trajectory up to that point. As Will.i.Am explained, "we let the audience guide us at any level. The people do it for you…Performing is therapy for us. That's what it is. Performing, being able to travel and do what you love and to touch people, it kind of … your fears and worries are secondary, if that. They're third or fourth on the list once you put all these good things into place. You got to count your blessings, before you count your woes and problems."

Elaborating, Taboo explained that "it's good to be able to go all over the world from Australia to Japan to Germany and have these b-boys, graffiti artists, DJs, MCs, to share the same energy that's shared here in the States. It shows you how big and how broad hip-hop is. It's not just an urban thing, a Black thing, a Puerto Rican thing, it's now a universal thing." While the group was firmly established as a headliner by this point, based off the success of Elephunk, that success also provided them an opportunity to again showcase their cross-over credentials when the Rolling Stones asked the group to open on a handful of the rock legends' tour dates, an invitation the group eagerly but nervously accepted, with Will.i.Am recalling that "that's a challenge right there, dog. Like 'Oh yeah, you guys thought you could rock out?' Yeah. Yeah, we'll open up for these niggas. We had to…come with our best game."

In addition to touring, the group branched out into a variety of side ventures that took each into their own universe of artistic/commercial expression. Will.i.Am indulged in his longtime love for fashion design, which had preceded the forming of the Black Eyed Peas.

The former attendee of the Fashion Institute of Design in Los Angeles launched the denim fashion line i.am.Antik in partnership with Blue Holdings Inc. He joined scores of other successful hip-hop brands Jay-Z's Roc-A-Wear, Russell Simmons' Phat Farm, and P. Diddy's Sean Jean.

In commenting on his vision for his clothing line, Will explained that "I produce and write my own music, and the same creativity, energy and imagination I put into making music is the same creativity, energy and imagination I put into designing clothes. I am excited to collaborate with Antik to create a fresh remix of denim…I want to design the line and score it the way a composer scores a film and tour the collection like a band will tour an album. I want to make a fresh stylistic collection that everyone wants but that's limited and special to keep them looking for more…I fuse genres of music and I will fuse eras and styles of fashion. I want to launch and market the clothes in a way that has never been done, combining music and fashion."

Additional to his denim line, Will was also hired by the Hard Rock Hotel and Casinos to customize a line of employee uniforms casino dealers, front desk concierges, cocktail waitresses and bellmen. Will viewed the opportunity as "an exciting and challenging proposition that, given my background and own line, I was eager to accept…My goal was to create a look that exudes upscale Rock 'n Roll, leveraging the essence of the brand while contemporizing the staff's wardrobe to provide a more stylistic and fashion-forward appearance."

Beyond fashion design, Will's creative prowess was also eyed by the Snickers candy bar company, which hired him to produce and direct a handful of science-fiction film shorts for an online advertising campaign featuring the Peas. The campaign was called Instant Def, and was comprised of a series of digi-sodes.

"Go online to reach teens because that's where they spend most of their time," Snickers' senior marketing manager Vic Walia said of the campaign. "The choice of Will.i.Am, Fergie, Taboo and Apl.de.Ap to be our Instant Def heroes was easy…They are setting trends and breaking away from the clutter in the industry to really stand out amongst their peers…We wanted to communicate the Snickers' brand message in an authentic, credible and contagious way. The Instant Def digi-sodes allows us to do that."

Will, for his part, was attracted to the project because "I can make music, incorporate it into a film that's on the Internet…That was a very nice experience. I personally learned a lot filming it. It was just an idea at one point in time…"

Fergie, for her part, explained that "I was very attracted to this project because Snickers gave me creative freedom…I had always dreamed of being a comic book character. I've always had this thought in my head of what I wanted to do with it. And so then they came to me with this idea and I said I know what I want to do."

Capitalizing on the opportunity as one of several in which she expanded upon her acting resume, Fergie was also keeping quite busy with side projects including a starring role in the Quentin Tarantino/Robert Rodriguez double-feature film 'Grindhouse.' Of working with the legendary directors, Fergie explained that "Robert and Quentin are my dream team. It was very cool because they're like the yin and the yang. They bounce off each other really well. It's like Robert's the left-brainer and Quentin's the right-brainer. I would go over with Robert and he'd be strumming his guitar, writing the music, and he'd play me the scene I was working on with the spooky music that was underneath. It was all very stylized, which I loved. And then I'd get with Quentin, and we'd both spaz out together, we'd start talking all over each other and it would be a lot of fun. It's not a big role, but I was like a sponge soaking it up, I wanted to learn… I tend to be attracted to dark, demented things. I love blood, guns, and knives. I like to play with my dark side…I play a girl named Tammy. It's not a big role. I didn't know Quentin was going to be there, because I'm in Robert's part of the film. Quentin showed up and worked with me on a scene in which I'm being chased. I was running, and Quentin was acting it out with me. At one point he put on a mask and attacked and bit me. They had to redo the scene about 10 times because he kept making all these noises. He bit and bruised me. He gets into the characters. He's amazing… When we started the film, the entire cast went to Quentin's house and they'd put together a montage of films, most of which I'd never seen before, of what they wanted the tone and rhythm of the movie to be."

Off the film set, Fergie was busy in the studio, writing her debut solo LP with Will and a host of other big name producers. Will continued to log hundreds of hours in the studio as one of the industry's most in-demand producers. He also found time in 2005 to work with the Peas on their fourth album, 'Monkey Business,' scheduled for release in 2006.

Given the well-earned opportunities coming the BEP's way after years of clawing and climbing their way from obscurity to the top, Will, in reflection, seemed to feel a sense of vindication.

"It's been a long journey to get here," he said. "Eazy-E passing away, being homeless…but we stuck to our dreams, and the community who gave us a hard time for what we did are coming to you to produce their records. Journalists fed us to the wolves, wrote us off, and those artists, those journalists are now applauding us. I'm proud of sticking to my guns."

The group's solo endeavors helped to advance the group's brand, Will explained. "We all help each other…Black Eyed Peas is the franchise. At the same time, we all launch off and do other things and always come back to Black Eyed Peas."

With the bar set high, the Black Eyed Peas headed into 2006 with the industry firmly behind it. That support allowed them to raise the stakes even higher, personally, and more ambitiously for hip-hop. The Peas emerged as one of game's biggest renaissance players. With its foundation firmly intact, the group looked forward to creating a little 'Monkey Business' in the coming year…

Part XII:
The Making of Monkey Business (2005)

"As a result of the international atmosphere and flavor during recording sessions, the BEP's fourth and most highly-anticipated studio LP trumped anything .... I like it better than 'Elephunk.'"

—Will.i.A.m

As global-locals of the international touring circuit and bonafide recording stars by the start of 2006, the BEP hadn't taken a pit stop in years. Arguably the most tireless advocate of the group's racing-pace, Will, felt anything less than the aforementioned momentum would compromise the band's greater chances for super-stardom. Between promoting 2003's 'Elephunk' to multi-platinum heights, producing countless hits of an equal caliber for the biggest names among his peers in the industry, designing clothing lines, and completing a host of other cross-branding business, Will still found time to write the group's fourth studio LP, 'Monkey Business.' Themed around the group's constant grind, Will drew the first contrast between this and prior BEP albums as being "that there was not a lot of fucking-around time."

Elaborating conceptually, he explained that "the idea with 'Monkey Business' was like organ grinders...You're working out there, and you only get a peanut, and you give all the money made to the monkey owner. There is a good payoff, but you work hard. Last week, we flew from South Africa to L.A. It was a 20-some-hour flight. And before that, we flew from Pittsburgh to Rome to Johannesburg, like, in five days. In Rome, we sat in traffic for, like, four hours, got to the hotel, washed up, went shopping, sat in traffic for two hours, went back, left the hotel to go to the MTV Europe awards show, four more hours of traffic, then went to an after-party for two hours and then left to get on a plane. I sound like a dick to say that it's hard, but it is hard on your body when you are on three hours of sleep...This album was made on my laptop on airplanes. At the time, we were traveling the world on 'Elephunk.' 'Where is the Love?', 'Let's Get Retarded' and 'Hey Mama' was huge all over the planet. We were doing shows in Vietnam, Lithuania, Brazil, Japan, South Korea, Philippines—all over the planet. I was thinkin' like 'When are we gonna make a record? 'Cause if we keep touring, we'll never make a record.' So I was doing it on the airplane, trying to feed the whole market at the same time. I wanna make an album that's gonna have songs that are relevant to every single country we are hitting at once."

Continuing, Will explained that "we're always open for challenges...You never know what situations you're going to be in and the demands you're going to have to meet—the vibe that you're in to even have the headspace to step up to that request. We're one of those groups that, whatever the obstacle is, we're going to put our best foot forward and figure out the way across it, under it, over it, or through it." Commenting for her own part, band mate Fergie explained that the group drew upon "all this creative energy...We wanted to spill it out and go with it. It was hard for me to get used to writing and recording on the road, because usually I'm doing studio time all at once, and then touring all at once. This was a big challenge, but it turned out to be this creative waterfall which just fell down into this huge ocean that is Monkey Business."

A truly international affair, the BEP's home hub for recording during tour stints was in London at Sting's state-of-the-art home studio. "We lived in London for two months while we toured Europe...We would fly back and forth on weekends—to Finland, Germany and France—and record during the week. And, along the way, we recorded in Brazil, Japan and Australia as well." Elaborating further on the group's routine when they were in London recording, Alp.de.Ap recalls that "we stayed in a house together...We'd cook in the morning and then hit the studio—well, Will was always in the studio."

The biggest treat for Will was "staying at Sting's house, where they had a farm with chickens and stuff! Being away from L.A. was being a kid off school for the summer. It wasn't like I didn't know what to do with myself—I had such a wild time!"

As a result of the international atmosphere and flavor during recording sessions, Will felt the BEP's fourth and most highly-anticipated studio LP trumped anything they had released prior, reasoning that 'Monkey Business' was "fresh, it's dope, and seriously, I'm not just saying it 'cause it's ours...I like it better than 'Elephunk.'"

Will characterized the vibe of the new album as "real aggressive...with edgier sounds, different polyrhythms and syncopations... We've always been all over the place...pulling real eclectic influences from music. We just love all forms of music, so this Monkey Business is like bossa nova to drum'n'bass to surf rock to hip-hop, mad all over the place...For instance, we fused Lisa Lisa with Bollywood and Miami bass...So that's a whole new, different sound." Fergie chimed in, calling it nostalgic. "You go back to songs that you experienced things with," she said.

Thematically, the producer explained that "the majority of the songs are about female relationships, turmoil, improvement, both personally and socially." Contrasting the atmosphere during recording sessions—in spite of their multiple physical locations—Will explained that for their new LP, "we wanted to have fun while recording in the studio. 'Elephunk' was recorded with that same spirit. We were just writing songs we could play live and dance to. The same with 'Monkey Business.' But this time we had new experiences. Artists should never chase success, just chase down their ideas, and have fun."

In examining the technical end of accomplishing the aforementioned task, Will described a truly mobile studio environment wherein "we have a portable studio that I take on the road...We record in airplanes, trains, hotel rooms, cathedrals. If we wanted to sneak in Notre Dame, we'd record up in that."

Elaborating on other skills Will felt he'd expanded as a producer in the years between writing and producing 'Elephunk' and 'Monkey Business,' he explained that "the more you stay around instruments, equipment, and musicians, your execution and skills will expand, leading to a different way of expression, and that has an effect on the outcome and sound. I am so happy with our growth. And can't wait to grow more,

One vocal recording tool Will took heavy advantage of while recording on the road was the Synchro Arts TDM VocALign plug-in, which the producer explained, using 'Don't Fuck With My Heart' as an example, that during the song's chorus features a unique robotic vocal effect "that is me and the sitar...When I sung it, I sung it in the same twang that the sitar was playing in, and then I put them together using VocALign...Or, say, for instance, you go do a rap, and it's off beat...But I liked your voice and the texture of your voice. What do I do? Okay, let me rap it, play it on time, get yours that's off time and VocAlign it to my time...So people who can't rap right, I'm just like, 'Nah, just say whatever you're going to say! I can make you say it.'...It's helped me out with a lot of shit—drummers, guitarists. Say, for instance, the guitarist's got a problem playing on the one. The rhythm is ducka ducka ducka dun ducka dun, but he's going ducka dun ducka dun; it's like, 'Just play it.' And then I'll record myself just hitting the rhythm on this desk. I tap out the rhythm and VocAlign his rhythm to my rhythm."

Another tool Will utilized to edit-as-he-recorded was the Serato Pitch 'n Time plug-in. "I have a conga sample, and the way that I got the live dude in to replay the sample just sounds like Guitar Center...I can't get it to sound like the way that it does on the sample. But the sample is in the key of E. The song is in C. So I Pitch 'n Time it to make it fit."

Part XIII:
Monkey Business Pt. II
B.E.P. Mix it Up with the King of
Pop and the Godfather of Soul

"With James Brown, you have history… He's the godfather of everything…Working with Mr. Brown was unlike anything words can explain."

—*Will.i.A.m*

The BEP took advantage of their contender status to recruit James Brown, the Godfather of Soul, for a collaboration on 'Monkey Business.' Famously savvy, Brown accepted, knowing his presence on the highly-anticipated album—as well as the press that it would generate—would work in his favor. The industry veteran needed a hook to help draw a new generation of listeners, especially among the hip-hop crowd. For the Peas, it was an opportunity to work with one of the most influential music men of all time. Indeed, Brown laid the foundation for most musical genres, including hip-hop, and outrageous stage performances.

"A lot of rappers wanna work with James Brown," Will recalled. "The thing is, he does not wanna work with them. We were in London at an awards show. I walked up to James Brown. I said, 'Thank you for all that you did for hip-hop. You may not know it or realize it, but hip-hop would not be what it is, without it.' So, I asked him the most daring question, 'You think we could do a song with you?' He said, 'Send me a reference for what you want me to do, and I'll do it.' "

Interestingly, as a footnote of irony, another of the reasons Brown agreed to work with the BEP was the same reason they had gotten flak from hip hop loyalists in the earlier years of their career, Will said.

"He pulls me aside and he says," Will said of Brown, " 'Ya know, Mr. Will, I don't got to work with nobody. But something tells me to work with the Black Eyed Peas. But I like how y'all do what y'all do. Y'all got the band. In hip-hop, music you don't see enough of that.' " Brown was also attracted to Will's gifts as a songwriter, with the BEP frontman recalling of their initial meeting that "he said 'I appreciate the fact that you took the time to write songs like, 'Where is the Love?' That's brave."

Among the lessons Will took from the time he spent with Brown, even ahead of entering the studio, the producer explains what he felt to be the most important—in context of the Black Eyed Peas—was one where "it was a history lesson to sit 'round James Brown, for him to say 'I like the Black Eyed Peas. You guys remind me of what we were doing back in the day' ...And to just sit there and talk to him about what black America was like in the '60s. What was black America like in the '70s? What's the difference between urban culture now and urban culture then? James said, 'People ain't got nuthin' to fight for. Back then we were fightin' for something, and it reflected in the music. People educated themselves to music theory. People played in church. Nowadays, people ain't fightin' for nuthin.' "

Continuing, Will recalled feeling so inspired by the experience that "I sat and couldn't help but interview him, asking him about everything from Malcolm X to Martin Luther King, to what black America felt like then compared to now, to music theory, to church, to men's suits...he educated me and gave me his blessing, saying how I reminded him of a son...So, we started talking. I started talking to him about Malcolm X, Martin Luther King Jr. and Elijah Muhammad. He knew all of them personally..."

Upon entering the studio to collaborate, the aforementioned term took on such complete definition that Will.i.Am and Brown actually sat down to write together, as opposed to Will crafting and composing the entire track ahead of the soul legend arriving just to record his vocals—as is common in such collaborations in hip-hop.

"We had the hook and the verse," Will said of songwriting with Brown, "and he came in with his part: 'You got to roll with the funk!' " Elaborating more broadly upon the session, Fergie remembered that "he came back and said, 'James Brown loves the Black Eyed Peas,' and Brown came to the studio on Monday...entourage and all. Everyone dressed to the nines. His hair—no hair out of place. He's got his background singers, his horn section. We did it all old-school. The way they used to do it. We got everyone in the room. It was crazy! Crazy!"

Together, the crews joined to write and record 'They Don't Want the Music,' an experience that Will summarized by pointing out that the singer's importance—both personally and professionally to broader hip-hop—was one based on history.

"With James Brown, you have history," Will said. "He's the godfather of everything…Working with Mr. Brown was unlike anything words can explain." So successful was the collaboration in the studio that Brown topped it off for the band by performing subsequently with them on stage, the ultimate compliment and acknowledgement of respect Will.i.Am felt the soul legend could have shown the group, explaining that "we had to do a benefit in Los Angeles, I called him a week before to come perform and he showed up. His manager was like, 'He does not do this for anybody.'… Our collaboration with James Brown was an accomplishment for hip-hop, seeing that what hip-hop sampled was based on James Brown, and yet no other groups have ever collaborated with him…we are blessed."

Elaborating further on the host of guest stars the group's clout had hooked them for the new LP. Fergie explained that "we're so excited with the success of 'Elephunk' that we thought, 'Wow, we actually have a chance … to work with these people who are legends to us?'…If you don't do it now, when are you going to do it?" In reviewing the experience of working with some of the album's other super-star collaborators, Fergie cites Sting, with whom the group teamed up for the track 'Union,' as a situation where "he came in, he wasn't even expecting to write and Will said, 'Why don't you flip something on the track?'…So he came up with some of the most beautiful lyrics on the album, I think – 'I'd change the world if I could change my mind.' It just came spontaneously, which is how our records are made anyway. So it was perfect."

Expanding further, Will.i.Am recalled that when "Sting shows up at the studio…he's like, 'What do you want me to do?'…So we asked him, 'Do you want to write a verse?' He said, 'Oh, you don't know what you're doing yet?' So we said, 'We're collaborating—to one of your songs.'…The message in that song is everybody getting together and uniting, the way that music comes together…We don't enjoy music that's out of key, so why do we live life out of key?" Another head-turning collaboration was the group's with folk rocker Jack Johnson, whose 'Gone, Gone, Gone,' the BEPs re-mixed.

"Jack Johnson actually wrote the entire song for himself and put it on his record," 'Fergie recalled. "So, Will went back to him and went, 'But it's also good this way. Why don't we treat it like a sample?' " Will, for his part, explained that "there's a song where we re-hashed something that Jack and I worked on in 2001…We kind of took one of his songs he had recorded…and fused it with what we originally did, scratched it and mixed as if we never met Jack…We looked at it, put it on vinyl and scratched it and treated it as a sample."

One familiar face on the LP was pop star Justin Timberlake, teaming with the BEPs in a sequel to their 2003 success with 'Where Is the Love?' For their new collaboration on 'My Style,' Will explained: "that song we did with Justin, that was a true collaboration…Not that the other ones weren't, but that was done from scratch. We just had the beat to start with. Timbaland popped the beat, and then Justin was like, 'Yo, you trying to get down on another song?' I said, 'As a matter of fact, Timbaland gave me a beat, you want to write to it?'… He's a friend…cool as shit…a homie."

In discussing some of the album's other tracks, Will explained that "the second single is a song called 'Don't Lie,' but at the same time we release that, we're gonna come with another lifestyle kind of song called 'Like That' with Q-Tip, Talib Kweli, John Legend and Cee-Lo…It's a summer feel-good song about messed up relationships…It's a song about owning up and apologizing and realizing your faults. It's about being a man, or a woman- an adult—and confronting situations honestly." In discussing the meaning behind some of the album's other tracks, Will turns to 'Like That' as "more underground hip-hop, where our roots came from," while 'Pump It,' Taboo explains works because "I like the energy it presents on stage. We've performed it a couple of times, and it gets the same reaction as 'Let's Get Retarded.' "

With a typically grueling touring schedule preceding the album's release, the BEP had a 34-date tour as co-headliners of the annual Honda Civic Tour that began in March 2006. The wildly popular Pussycat Dolls would open the tours at the conclusion of the tour in May. Will was pleased with the lineup. The "Pussycat Dolls really come wit' it...I think they rock routines better than any other group I ever seen do routines, 'cause I personally hate routines...But they really put the personality beyond the routine." Having just come off a co-headlining tour with Gwen Stefani in 2005, the Peas had officially arrived.

Elaborating more broadly on his own expectations for BEP shows in context of both audience satisfaction and longevity, Will explained that "all the tours that happened in 2005, the 50 Cent/ Eminem tour, as big as those artists are, it wasn't like as crazy as you think it was gonna be saleswise…So for us, to build that Dave Matthews-type of touring awareness, that no matter what song we have on the radio we can still go out and tour, we still have to put in work in the States. We've been putting in work all over the planet but we haven't put in our work in the States yet."

Focusing on the band's visual performance aspect of their songs as much as the musical delivery, Will revealed that as part of the BEP's planning stages, "we've had long conversations about who we gonna bring, what's smart, what aesthetically is cool. We just have to think about it and do it right…I'm excited about going out in the States and doing our own thing in our own venues, our own stage, people there for us…When we go on the road again…it will be all Monkey Business."

Released on June 7th, 2005, Monkey Business debuted at No. 2 on Billboard's Top 200 Album Chart with sales of 291,000 copies, their highest debut to date, reflecting the anticipation the group's fans were feeling toward the group's latest album. It would go onto sell 9 million copies worldwide, producing hits, including 'Don't Phunk With My Heart,' 'My Humps' which reached No. 1 on the Billboard Hot 100 Singles Chart, and 'Don't Lie.' The group received four Grammy Award nominations in 2006 for which they won Best Rap Performance By a Duo or Group for 'Don't Phunk With My Heart.' 'My Humps' won for the 'Best Pop Performance by a Duo or Group with Vocal' at the 2007 Grammy Awards.

In reflecting on the group's massive crossover success, he felt they had come full-circle with the LP, explaining that "Bridging the Gap was the plan: 'We see a big gap here, and I wanna bridge it.' I wanna build a bridge for the people on the desert to come and get water at the lake. After that bridge was made: 'Elephunk.' We rode our elephants over the bridge! Then when we realized all the politics and how much the elephant weighed, we were like, 'Yo, man, this business is kind of wack. This is like Monkey Business.'…The whole

thing was a documentary of our travels...It just totally opened my mind up to 'Monkey Business.'"

In terms of crediting any one thing to the BEP's success, Will felt the group was very much the sum of their individual parts, reasoning that " 'Monkey Business' is the manifestations of all our experiences, thoughts, and creative visions...Each member of the Peas brings themselves to the table. And with that comes their ideas, inspirations, and experiences...and we each bring some personality differences as well. Ferg is just beautiful in every way possible, apl is humble and heart driven, Taboo is fire, passion and energy, and I am always thinking and trying to build, and move, like let's go!! 'I got an idea,' that's my favorite phrase."

Will concluded his reflections on the success of the group's latest smash hit LP by reflecting on how it measured how far the group had come, such that, as far as the B.E.P. producer/founder was concerned, "all these things that we're doing right now are a reward. If you really want to achieve in life, change yourself and aim for it." The only question now was how much higher could the group climb as the millennium continued to unfold? For Fergie, her next ascension up the chart of pop royalty would come as a solo artist, with the debut of her first starring LP, 'The Dutchess of York...'

Part XIV:
Fergie Ferg
The Dutchess of York
(2006-2007)

"We didn't see her group perform, but a friend of mine suggested setting her up for a song on our third record, 'Elephunk' in 2003, and he was like, 'Trust me, she can sing her ass off.' So she came to the studio, and I was like, 'You hear our harmony?' She was like, 'Which one—the third or fifth?' I was like, 'Wow!' I mean, she came in with knowledge! She came in and was just knocking it out in, like, 30 minutes. We work pretty fast—our thing is to capture the moment as quick as possible."

—Will.i.Am

As perhaps the brightest star—commercially speaking—in the BEP's constellation, Fergie's solo album was simply inevitable as 2006 approached. In spite of the Black Eyed Peas' success, Fergie felt her solo LP was as a growth opportunity, given that "I always had this dream. I told my mom when I was 7 years old, but I just ended up being in bands. I'm a free spirit. I follow my heart, and it's led me to where I am now. I probably would've taken more time to finish it even though they're songs from a seven-year period. But Interscope Records CEO Jimmy Iovine heard some tracks and was like, 'This is great, let's put it out'."

The band was in agreement on the timing, understanding that this had been part of the singer's plan from the start, explaining for her part that "it wasn't the plan that I was going to be in the Black Eyed Peas—that just sort of happened organically because we started working together musically and became really good friends. It's been my life's dream to have a solo record. It just took awhile to get there. I was always in bands. It's my time to spread my wings. "I had been a fan of theirs since 1998... I first saw the Peas at the El Ray Theater in Los Angeles... They were amazing dancers and MCs with this sick style, and I... I knew right away I wanted to work with them...One of the last shows I did with Wild Orchid-this is after I knew that I was leaving, I was just fulfilling my commitment-BEP were on the bill. It wasn't like they were the No. 1 artists at the time or anything. I was finally doing my own album, and I knew that crossing paths with them must mean something—I felt like it was a sign. I knew it was hip-hop with a very eclectic twist, which is what I was inspired by...I approached Will in the hallway, got my hustle on and exchanged numbers. We started playing phone tag and having conversations. They needed a singer for 'Shut Up,' and we started working together but we didn't plan to be a band. I was still working on my solo material with Will, becoming friends with the guys and doing background on their albums. When it came time for them to tour with 'Elephunk,' I was a background staple. Joining a band was another commitment, but I was such a huge fan of theirs, and I thought I'd be an even better solo artist if I learned from them."

Fergie worked to distinguish her sound from the Peas—despite the fact that Will was the producer of her album.. "It is different because I'm a singer first and foremost," said the artist who is on Will's label. "There are more ballads and more intimacy between me and the listener because sometimes when you're in a group, you don't have space to air out your dirty laundry. This album is a complete thought. It's not just a verse or a sentence. It's my complete feeling and emotion. I think people will be surprised because they don't know that sensitive side of me yet. I also like to experiment with different tones in my voice, and I wanted to make the album really colorful."

Will further explained of the group's support for Fergie's solo outing that, "We're really proud and supportive. We're going to tour together. It doesn't make sense for her to open up for other people when she's in one of the biggest groups in the world. So we'll tour together, still record together, we have a Black Eyed Peas album coming in 2007. But right now it's 'Dutchess' time."

One of Fergie's chief aims with the album's perfectly-balanced mix of melodic singing and hip-hop was to pay homage to her childhood love of both cultures. Beginning with the former style, Fergie cited some of her chief female vocal influences as "Lauryn Hill—I wish she would come out with another album, she was such an amazing artist, and she also came out of a guy band, and India.Arie because she was just so strong about her inner self. The same thing with Jill Scott, and Alanis Morissette. I think she was an amazing artist. She wasn't afraid to take risks and be who she was. There definitely was no Alanis Morissette before Alanis Morissette. You make your own rules. I think that's another reason to get my album—there are no rules on it. I'm not trying to conform to any one style or any particular radio market. It's just really representative of who I am, and the artists I love the most are the ones who are really honest."

In turning to hip-hop artists, Fergie was equally as enthusiastic, explaining that her love for it had grown out of "just being around it and living the lifestyle with the BEP. It felt more natural and comfortable—and not as taboo. But I've always been a fan of rappers like Roxanne Shante, Monie Love, Queen Latifah, Salt-N-Pepa… because those are like a lot of idols I had when I was younger, like Queen Latifah and all the female MCs—I also loved Whitney Houston and Mariah Carey, you know?…These were girls that I emulated growing up, but just more in private. BEP gave me that confidence to do it. I'm not trying to be a serious MC. That's not my goal. I'm just paying homage to everything I grew up listening to. If I didn't include that part of me, it wouldn't be a true representation of who I am."

Shedding light on the genesis of her stage name, Fergie explained that "it's a family nickname. My sister Dana is Ferg. We all go by different variations. It's a common nickname for the last name. Fergie was actually going to be used for the name of a solo album, but then I joined the Black Eyed Peas. It was kind of a rebirth for me because I had gotten off drugs and it was a new start."

Fulfilling her ultimate childhood dream with her solo album, Fergie explained that "I've known…and been wanting to do this ever since I was a little girl…I told my mom 'I'm going to have a solo album.' And she said, 'Fine, as long as you get good grades.'…So it's just a beautiful thing, it's my lifetime project…It's gonna be more personal and a deeper look into who I am as a person, more vulnerable than I am with the Peas."

In training as a performer and vocalist since the age of 7, Fergie explained that her ability to rap and sing with equal personality came from having "done voiceovers all my life…I was Sally for 2 years and then Lucy for one year on 'Charlie Brown' among other characters. I like to play with different voices, which is what I'm having a lot of fun doing on this record...I got a chance to be in front of a microphone at 8 years old and learn harmonies singing with Rahsaan Patterson, who was my vocal idol at the time. I always wanted his voice."

Socially, Fergie's days on the set of 'Kids Incorporated'- among such other child stars as Martika, Jennifer Love Hewitt, and Shanice- provided her with an additional opportunity to expand her musical pallet. "We used to listen to Chaka Kahn and Prince, and watch movies like Breakin'— 1984 and Sid and Nancy—1986," She recalled. She drew from the inspirational well of her childhood musical and cultural influences, as well as from her whirlwind days of partying and performing with Wild Orchid, including a brutal recovery from her addition to Crystal Meth.

Truly feeling redeemed through the writing and recording of her solo LP, Fergie explained that its evolution began from "when I left my mom's house to go out on tour with the Peas. I was collecting unemployment and just hustling to get my demos made... I chose to start doing right and really just got my hustle on, using my air miles to fly around and meet with producers so I could make some demos...I was still struggling to get into studios—even home studios—wherever I could work with people whose music I liked and record some demos...I always knew when I was a kid that this is what I wanted to do. It took a while, but I did it...So this has all been a huge blessing since I didn't know what was going to happen."

In entrusting her dream to an executive producer to help in guiding it to sonic reality, Fergie tapped BEP mastermind Will.i.Am, who she felt "he's like my partner in crime... We get in the studio and sometimes we'll disagree and sometimes we'll really agree, but we just have such a love relationship. We just understand each other. I mean the first time we worked together, on the song 'Shut Up,' we got the song done in less than an hour. I could say something that won't make sense to the normal ear, but he'll understand...My plan in the beginning was to work with Will. I just stuck by it. It was also convenient because we were on tour and I had to finish the album. We had a bus with a recording studio, so a few hours before we went on stage we could go in and get some stuff done. I felt pressured at the end because I had a deadline. If it were up to me, I'd still be working on it, but Jimmy Iovine, the head of Interscope Records, heard some songs and wanted to put it out. You can't argue with him…Will is such a great musical encyclopedia. I've learned so much from being in the studio with him and talking to him…I'm on the campaign for him to be producer of the year."

Will viewed his greatest challenge heading into the collaboration as "the same shit as everyone else…thought—'What are we going to do different?'…Then when you get in there, you start making the songs and you start finding the groove, and it's totally different. It's not different to where it ain't the same person in the crew; you got to still keep that familiarity. But the singing, the melodies, it's a breath of fresh air. She has a great voice and it's prominent throughout the record…Her personality doesn't switch up. She's still Fergie, but, it's just more about her…There's more melodies I have to think about, it's way more melodic. It was hard, because we were recording the record while we were touring."

Recorded simultaneously as 'Elephunk' and 'Monkey Business,' Fergie took advantage of the group's residence in the John Lennon Studio Bus to knock out tracks, with the singer recalling that "we'd go in a couple of hours before going on stage and that's how it got done. The songs span a seven-year period. Some were done before I was in the Black Eyed Peas-we just updated them, and some were done in this one-month span that we took off from touring, which is very rare for us."

Elaborating on the pace of recording, producer Will.i.Am explained that "a lot of people don't realize, but I was producing her by mid-2002, writing songs with her and, at the same time, we were recording 'Elephunk.' We've been trying to figure out the release since. Should we put it out after Elephunk? No, we still need to work as the Black Eyed Peas. We set the anchor. No matter what happened with the individual projects, we committed to the Peas… We recorded in London…We recorded in Beijing. We recorded in Australia. We recorded in- what's another weird place? 'Clumsy' was recorded in the John Lennon bus—a traveling music education lab, like in a parking lot in Pittsburgh right next to Shakey's…To be able to record on the road, that's a task and a half…We've recorded all over the world—Australia, Beijing, London, Paris, Canada, America, Mexico…And this project has been so important to me to stand alongside Fergie and record in the studio."

When not on the road, Fergie was still hard at work on the album, recalling that "Will and I moved into this studio house in Malibu called Morningview. It's like a ranch. It was very serene-complete opposite to the chaos of touring. I was alone a lot, which is something that doesn't happen to me on tour, so I got to find these emotions that are a little bit deeper than the surface." Elaborating more indepthly on her writing method, Fergie explained that "I couldn't have written songs today that I wrote five years ago because I wasn't feeling that. So that's why I'm really excited about this. It's just a mixture of emotions on this record…And it's very autobiographical. All of the love songs are definitely about different boyfriends that I've had. I've made a personal decision to not mention which ones are about who out of respect for the people. But there are breakups, there are make-ups, there are dysfunctional relationships. There are also struggles with my substance abuse, a lot of vulnerability which I think people haven't seen from me in the Black Eyed Peas… Every song has its own character…They use different pieces of my voice and that's what I want to express, 'cause it's fun. It makes the album less boring for me and hopefully for others as well."

In the interest of keeping her fans' ears as attentive as their eyes were used to seeing her perform on stage, Fergie explained that she and Will produced "a very colorful album…There's dub, there's reggae, there's stuff like the Temptations, a band that I saw when I was 10 years old in concert. There's the low rider, oldie style that we revisit that I was really inspired by in high school. There's that punk-rock aspect—that just really raw rock and roll, get your hair messed up, sweat as much as you want, don't feel pretty on stage—that aspect. There's jazzy. We're just crazy." Still, while in the studio, Fergie explained the atmosphere was all-business so much so that "when you work with him (Will), it is work," she recalled. "I'm also just very serious when it comes to this stuff—it's a no-bullshit situation. It's about, 'Okay, this is not a fun thing that passes the time. It's a lifelong dream of mine.'"

Focusing on the finished album in specific, Fergie began by addressing the conceptual reasons behind the album's royal title. " 'The Dutchess' is a play on words from the Duchess of York, but it's not to be taken literally. If you notice, on the album cover it says 'Fergie as the Dutchess' because I wanted each song to be a movie poster. But because 'London Bridge' did so well so fast, only half the songs on the album have movie poster themes." Addressing her smash hit, 'London Bridge,' the album's lead single, Will.i.Am explained that it had grown from another of the Peas' biggest hits, 'My Humps.' "I

didn't want to give it away to anyone else," Will said. "I wrote it for the Pussycat Dolls, but then I said, 'I want to keep this bad boy for us. Hey, Fergie, you wanna sing this?' We would never have originally sung that. But doing that song kinda gave birth to a whole new Fergie character, a side of something that she could have fun with. And it kinda introduced that whole thing: sing-a-long, sing-songy fun music. That song opened the door for the 'London Bridges' song."

Elaborating on the song's thematic meaning, Fergie explained that "there are a couple things that you could relate with that title, but I'm just going to leave it to people's imagination." Addressing the rapping the song required her to put on tape, the singer revealed that she found it "funny, because I'm a singer and this single doesn't have a lot of singing to it…It's more of a chanty type of record, but it just seemed so obvious that it would be the first single, because it was so strong and aggressive. I'm just excited for people who hear the whole record, because there's going to be a lot of different styles on the record. I have very eclectic taste, just as the Black Eyed Peas do…'London Bridge' and 'Fergalicious' were definitely more surface songs…I have a very serious side as well, and it's completely different, and you don't know whether people are going to embrace that or not." Sticking with the album's lighter fare for the moment, Fergie discussed another of the album's singles, 'Fergalicious,' which she explained as "kind of a throwback to J.J. Fad. 'Fergalicious' is…based on…when I went to Knott's Berry Farm in California and did what I thought was a dance battle…In 'Fergalicious,' I emulated J.J. Fad, and we sampled the track from Afro-Rican's 'Give It All You Got.'" Other hip-hop tracks Will.i.Am recalls working on included " 'Big Girls Don't Cry,' really pushed my production skills. I did an Edie Brickell type of production—'I'm not aware of too many things,' on guitars. 'Clumsy' is like the Shangri-Las 'Leader of the Pack,' with a ghetto-ass beat, but then here come the guitars and her singers."

Other hip-hop collaborations on the album included Ludacris appearing on 'Glamorous,' and Cypress Hill's B Real on 'Thrilla Man,' a re-make of the rap group's classic, 'How I Could Just Kill a Man,' who said of his collaboration with Fergie that "it's pretty hot…Basically she took the song and switched the story around to suit it to her and put the female touch on it. She did the same chorus, she even did my same rhyme style, but she sung it. It's hard to describe it, you just got to hear it—she did it justice."

One guest whose presence on the LP was especially personal to Fergie was that of Bob Marley's widow, Rita Marley on the track 'Mary Jane's Shoes,' which the singer explained "was quite an honor for me…We recorded a beautiful reggae song…I kind of get to play Bob Marley in that song, which is a beautiful thing…Its a breezy reggae song, and at the end I go into a little bit of punk-rock mosh music." Will.i.Am, in elaborating on the song's production, explained that Fergie "goes from dub, doing her interpretation of roots, to some ska-punk and ends up with jazz. From a production standpoint that was fun, flipping all those different styles."

Another of Fergie's favorites was, 'Here I Come,' which she explained contained "a Temptations sample in it. It's a beautiful song—just a classic throwback to the old school with a bit of modern hip-hop involved. I would love for you to hear 'Clumsy.' It's kind of a throwback to '60s pop—a modernized version of that. I do a little speech, like the Shangri-Las did in their songs. The vernacular of it very much pays homage to that period." Fergie's album, which reflects her wide array of musical derivatives, also contained 'Voodoo Doll,' which she saw as "my take on dub music. It's about my struggle with Crystal Meth. There's a demon part that's a completely different voice than the singing part, and it's almost like two voices. It's me battling with myself…In these songs…what I'm really talking about in…'Voodoo Doll' is about the temptation of it and the struggle of good and evil. Then 'Losing My Ground' is about where I ended up and the desperation I felt. It really goes into detail. These are definitely songs that are autobiographical, but so are the other ones."

On another single, she collaborated with John Legend on 'Finally,' a ballad. Fergie described it as a timeless ballad that listeners will enjoy 30 years from now. "It'll still be cool because it doesn't lend to any era," she said. "And it's really stripped down…It was something that the record really needed, a simple, classic, timeless ballad…I really had a chance to sing, although I didn't over-sing anything. My taste is more to bring it out at certain moments." Other songs on the softer side, include 'The Makeup Song All That I Got' and 'Velvet.' "I wanted the latter to sound like velvet feels-very smooth-and I wanted it to be sensual."

Upon completion of the principle tracking on the album, Will felt the duo had crafted a masterpiece. In terms of commercial appeal, the producer was convinced that Fergie had enough of a variety to please all of her demographics. "She'll have a song about voodoo dolls, where she's talking about her past, and getting over those demons, but then she'll have a song like 'Fergalicious,' where it's just being sassy and flaunting her stuff from a strong female perspective, paying homage to Salt-N-Pepa."

In sum, Will clearly felt the album was as eclectically flavored as any BEP album, but still broke enough new ground to establish Fergie as a star in her own right. Where the latter balance had played a role in selecting the album's final track listing—versus those which wound up instead as BEP releases—Fergie explained a process by which "if something feels right for the Peas' album, it's going to make it...You don't save something that's perfect for the Black Eyed Peas just because you want to hold onto it." Will felt, in the end, that it didn't matter as one project was an extension artistically of the other, reasoning that "we're chameleons...We can open up for Metallica or go rock with Justin Timberlake. Or we could go out with Busta Rhymes. We have so many different types of—I want to say 'personalities,' but then you would think we're cuckoo—but we have so many different types of suits that we could put on and still be us."

Once the album was completed, Fergie began plotting out her world tour as a solo act and with the Peas. She confessed that it made her a little nervous to perform with the Peas. "I never really get nervous with the Peas because there are four of us and we perform the songs every night." she said. "But these songs, I haven't performed.

So it's harder because I'm still remembering all the lyrics and stuff. I like to be a little bit more sure of what I'm doing… I need a little bit more rehearsal time than the Peas do to feel comfortable. The Peas don't even rehearse! Even when I first joined the band, it was like, one time we spent four hours going through things, and that was it before I went on tour with them. It's a different thing, though, because you have four people carrying the show. With me alone, I just want to be a little bit more prepared because I have to hold the whole thing… I'm a risk taker…Still, I had fears all the way…I was nervous at first getting on stage without my guys…having a show be all my material. Now I'm getting more comfortable with it and I'm having fun with it."

On the road, Fergie adhered to a strict diet, with a rider of low-fat cottage cheese, bagels, freshly squeezed orange juice, soy milk, coffee, and water," she said. " I'm going to start trying to order more organic foods," she said. "I'm getting into that because I've got a trainer and she's inspiring me to get into all the non-processed foods. I'm starting to do my homework, it's my new project." Given that album was largely while touring abroad, Fergie hoped fans would also connect with the material on an international basis. "Touring the world, you're experiencing so many things and you're influenced by so many things that that is your truth," she reflected. "It wouldn't be honest if you didn't include all those influences in what you're doing."

When she is out on the town, either with friends or her fiancé— actor Josh Duhamel—Fergie explains that "it's just cool to go out for meals without worrying about the cost these days. It's a simple thing, but so nice. I used to save my money, but it didn't go very well. At one point, I spent everything I had and I had to move back home to live with my mom!…I'm not a diva. I really appreciate how lucky I am to be able to live the life I'm living. Being broke makes you really appreciate money 'cause you know you could lose it all in one day-that makes me humble."

One thing Fergie does find time to indulge in off the road is rest, explaining that "I treasure my sleep very much now…It's hard because I give everything to the band and we just came off the Canadian tour and that went amazing, but when I'm coming back here [to the set] it's a completely different life and I have to give myself fully to this, so I'm working two jobs right now, but it's cool. I love giving myself fully to something."

Released on September 19, 2006, 'The Dutchess of York,' bowed at No. 3 on the coveted Billboard Magazine Top 200 Album Chart, It went on to sell 2 million copies in the U.S., and almost 4 million worldwide. 'London Bridge,' a single from the album soared to the top of the charts. The single's racy video also was popular on MTV.

In terms of the video, which Fergie shot on location in London, she explained its concept as one where "we got to use the whole cheeky London-type thing, playing with the British guards…But at the same time, we were playing with the '60s London feel, with the Brigitte Bardot bouffant hair, and mixing that up with the chola style. It's kind of a weird fusion, and it somehow just all works together…People have never seen me in the Black Eyed Peas videos going to clubs and hanging out with my girls, and that's a big part of me…I love to go to clubs, hang out, get buck wild, get into fashion."

Other smash hit singles included 'Big Girls Don't Cry,' 'Glamorous,' featuring Ludacris, and 'Fergalicious.' The albums success prompted a huge promotional campaign, including talk show appearances. "It's been very surreal that 'London Bridge' has done so well. I've been on tour with the Black Eyed Peas, so for that song to become a number-one single is crazy for me. When I found out, I was walking around the house crying—happy tears."

The hard work and late nights was worth all of the effort. In who she feels she's trying to reach with the album, Fergie says she is trying to introduce herself to people who do not know her. "It's interesting because I feel like I'm very open and very honest in interviews and such, but I don't know if a lot of people know who I am or what I've been through and all the different phases of my life," she recalled. "The Black Eyed Peas' music is very party-oriented. In that context I don't know if people know the more intimate side of me, the romantic and sensual side. I wanted to let people in a bit more on this album. Next time I might do a reggae or hip-hop album—I don't know what I'll do, but for this album I wanted to get really personal with the audience."

Elaborating further still, the singer explained that, at its core, the album was "a deeper look into who I am. Soundwise…it is eclectic like the Peas but I…get to experiment with more of the different sounds of my voice. I like to use my voice as an instrument sometimes and I'll be able to show that on that album." In looking to the future, Fergie was sure first to thank her co-producer and bandmate Will.i.Am for "believing in me when I was living at my mom's and just really understanding that girl that was in suburbia and seeing something that was in her…Taboo, APL and Will.i.Am see me as a sister. They say that they always try to save me from the bad things and I appreciate it, as Will.i.Am was the one who persuaded me to give up drugs."

With so many opportunities brightly guiding her future, Fergie seemed to convey a resolve to keep both her career—and that of the BEP—moving forward as progressively, positively, and poignantly as ever before, explaining that "I think everything happens for a reason and all of my choices have led me up to this moment and made me stronger, not only as an artist but as a person. I want to do more BEP albums and more of my own albums. I'm in this for the long run."

Conclusion:
The Black Eyed Peas
(2008 and Beyond…)

"No PBS producer could assemble a more convincing multi-cultural cast—a black man, a white girl, a Mexican, a Filipino. And no A&R executive could contrive a sound that hits so many of sweet spots. During their tireless two-hour set, the Peas appropriate a Guns N' Roses riff, a Michael Jackson bassline here, and a hook from 50 Cent and Kelis there. The Black Eyed Peas' cheerful, cartoonish approach, far removed from most hip-hop's so-called realness, has made its members the world's favorite good-time rappers. Will has become one of the industry's most sought after songwriters and producers. Crossover superstars from Kanye West to Diddy praise the work of the Peas. Radio programmers and Fortune 500 marketing executives take comfort in their upbeat idealism. The group's come-together anthem, 'Where Is the Love?', featuring Justin Timberlake, was a global phenomenon in 2003. The following year, 'Let's Get Retarded'—tactfully renamed 'Let's Get It Started'—was the NBA's playoff them, and became burned in minds of basketball fans and couch potatoes from all-around.. Their 2003 album, 'Elephunk,' sold more than 7 million copies worldwide. Last year's follow-up, 'Monkey Business', has already passed the 4 million mark."

—Blender Magazine

Looking forward, the Peas plan to continue pushing the boundaries of music, especially hip-hop. The group headed into production of its fifth studio album with confidence. "Its easier now than it was in 1996," Will said. "But it's still that fear of losing that drive and motivation and determination now that you've accomplished something. That's what's scary to us...We're afraid of losing what got us here, and that was humbleness and hunger."

With the bar set high as ever, Will revealed as the summer of 2007 rolled along, that the group was hard at work in the studio with "12 songs...and we'll probably do another 30 or 40." Directionally, Will categorized the group's new album as "a thinking record. It brings up what's happening in the world. 'Monkey Business' didn't do that." Still, the BEP frontman was quick to point out to fans that "we are not complaining!"

With Will's own nomination in the spring for Producer of the Year, along with five other awards for the Peas, the future couldn't hold any more promise for the group. Will.i.Am's ultimate goals for the future of the group involves his unique brand of edutainment (education + entertainment). "We, as people, need to continue to spread that message. Continue to educate yourself on what's going on in Africa. People are dying of malaria and AIDS at a constant rate. People are dying all around the world because of world hunger every day, of malnutrition. Just educate yourself on world issues and everything will be straight!"

Black Eyed Peas Chart History

Studio Albums/Singles:

▼ *Behind the Front*

— Released: 1998
— Chart positions: #129 U.S.
— RIAA certification: N/A
— Worldwide sales: Over 200,000 worldwide
— Singles: "Head Bobs", "What It Is", "Karma", "Joints & Jams", "Fallin' Up"

▼ *Bridging the Gap*

— Released: 2000
— Chart positions: #67 U.S., #37 Australia
— RIAA certification: N/A
— Worldwide sales: Over 300,000 worldwide
— Singles: "Request + Line" (with Macy Gray), Peak Position: # 63 on the Billboard Top 100 Pop Chart,, "Get Original", "Weekends" (with Esthero), "BEP Empire"

▼ *Elephunk*

— Released: 2003
— Chart positions: #14 U.S., #3 UK, #1 Australia
— RIAA certification: 2x Platinum
— CRIA certification: 7x Platinum
— Worldwide sales: 10 million
— Singles: "Where Is the Love?" (with Justin Timberlake), Peak Position: # 8 on the Billboard Top 100 Pop Chart, "Shut Up", "Hey Mama" Peak Position: # 21 on the Billboard Top 100 Pop Chart,, "Let's Get It Started" Peak Position: # 23 on the Billboard Top 100 Pop Chart, "The APL Song"

▼ *Monkey Business*

— Released: 2005
— Chart positions: #2 U.S.; #4 UK; #1 Canada; #1 Australia
— RIAA certification: 3x platinum
— CRIA certification: 6x platinum
— Worldwide sales: 12 million
— Singles: "Don't Phunk with My Heart"- Peak Position: # 3 on the Billboard Top 100 Pop Chart, "Don't Lie" Peak Position: # 14 on the Billboard Top 100 Pop Chart, "Like That" (with Cee-Lo, Talib Kweli, John Legend & Q-Tip), "My Humps"- Peak Position: # 3 on the Billboard Top 100 Pop Chart, "Pump It"- Peak Position: # 18 on the Billboard Top 100 Pop Chart, "Bebot" (unofficial)

EPs:

▼ *Renegotiations: The Remixes* (March 21, 2006)

Grammy Award History:

Category	Genre	Song	Year
Best Pop Performance by a Duo or Group	Rap	"My Humps"	2005
Best Pop Performance by a Duo or Group	Rap	"Don't Phunk with My Heart"	2006
Best Rap Performance by a Duo or Group	Rap	"Lets Get it Started"	2005

Fergie Chart/Awards/Acting History:

▼ *The Dutchess*

- — Released: Released: September 19, 2006
- — Chart Position: # 3 US, # 27 UK, # 4 CA,
- — RIAA certification: 3x platinum
- — Worldwide: 3,800,000
- — Singles: "London Bridge" Peak Position: # 1 on the Billboard Top 100 Pop Chart, "Fergalicious" (Ftring. Will.i.Am), Peak Position: # 2 on the Billboard Top 100 Pop Chart, "Glamorous" (Ftring. Ludacris), Peak Position: # 1 on the Billboard Top 100 Pop Chart, "Big Girls Don't Cry", Peak Position: # 3 on the Billboard Top 100 Pop Chart

Black Eyed Peas

About the Author

Nashville-based music biographer **Jake Brown** is the author of fifteen published books, including *Red Hot Chili Peppers: In the Studio*; *Dr. Dre: In the Studio*; *Kanye West In The Studio: Beats Down! Money Up! (The Studio Years (2000-2006)*; *Tupac Shakur (2-Pac) In the Studio: The Studio Years (1987-1996)*; *50 Cent: No Holds Barred*; *Jay Z and the Roc-A-Fella Dynasty*; *Ready to Die: The Story of Biggie Smalls—Notorious B.I.G.*; *Your Body's Calling Me: The Life and Times of Robert "R" Kelly—Music, Love, Sex & Money*; and *Suge Knight: The Rise, Fall and Rise of Death Row Records*. Brown was also a featured author in Rick James' recently published autobiography, *Memoirs of a Super Freak: The Confessions of Rick James*. Brown is also owner of the hard rock label Versailles Records.

ORDER FORM

WWW.AMBERBOOKS.COM

Fax Orders: 480-283-0991

Telephone Orders: 480-460-1660

Postal Orders: Send Checks & Money Orders to:

Amber Books

1334 E. Chandler Blvd., Suite 5-D67, Phoenix, AZ 85048

Online Orders: E-mail: Amberbk@aol.com

_____*Black Eyed Peas: Unauthorized Biography,* ISBN 978-0-9790976-4-5, $16.95

_____*Red Hot Chili Peppers: In the Studio,* ISBN #: 978-0-9790976-5-2, $16.95

_____*Dr. Dre In the Studio,* ISBN#: 0-9767735-5-4, $16.95

_____*Kanye West in the Studio,* ISBN #: 0-9767735-6-2, $16.95

_____*Tupac Shakur—(2Pac) In The Studio,* ISBN#: 0-9767735-0-3, $16.95

_____*Jay-Z…and the Roc-A-Fella Dynasty,* ISBN#: 0-9749779-1-8, $16.95

_____*Your Body's Calling Me: The Life & Times of "Robert" R. Kelly,* ISBN#: 0-9727519-5-52, $16.95

_____*Ready to Die: Notorious B.I.G.,* ISBN#: 0-9749779-3-4, $16.95

_____*Suge Knight: The Rise, Fall, and Rise of Death Row Records,* ISBN#: 0-9702224-7-5, $21.95

_____*50 Cent: No Holds Barred,* ISBN#: 0-9767735-2-X, $16.95

_____*Aaliyah—An R&B Princess in Words and Pictures ,* ISBN#: 0-9702224-3-2, $10.95

_____*You Forgot About Dre: Dr. Dre & Eminem,* ISBN#: 0-9702224-9-1, $10.95

_____*Divas of the New Millenium,* ISBN#: 0-9749779-6-9, $16.95

_____*Michael Jackson: The King of Pop,* ISBN#: 0-9749779-0-X, $29.95

_____*The House that Jack Built (Hal Jackson Story),* ISBN#: 0-9727519-4-7, $16.95

Name:_____

Company Name:_____

Address:_____

City:_____State:_____Zip:_____

Telephone: (____) _____E-mail:_____

For Bulk Rates Call: **480-460-1660**   **ORDER NOW**

Black Eyed Peas	$16.95	❏ Check ❏ Money Order ❏ Cashiers Check
Red Hot Chili Peppers	$16.95	❏ Credit Card: ❏ MC ❏ Visa ❏ Amex ❏ Discover
Dr. Dre In the Studio	$16.95	
Kanye West	$16.95	
Tupac Shakur	$16.95	CC#_____
Jay-Z…	$16.95	Expiration Date:_____
Your Body's Calling Me:	$16.95	**Payable to:**
Ready to Die: Notorious B.I.G.,	$16.95	Amber Books
Suge Knight:	$21.95	1334 E. Chandler Blvd., Suite 5-D67
50 Cent: No Holds Barred,	$16.95	Phoenix, AZ 85048
Aaliyah—An R&B Princess	$10.95	
Dr. Dre & Eminem	$10.95	**Shipping:** $5.00 per book. Allow 7 days for delivery.
Divas of the New Millenium,	$16.95	**Sales Tax:** Add 7.05% to books shipped to Arizona addresses.
Michael Jackson: The King of Pop	$29.95	
The House that Jack Built	$16.95	**Total enclosed: $**_____